The Guide to the Architecture of Georgia

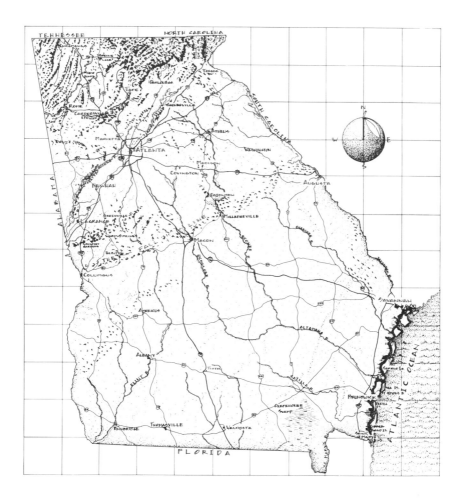

The Guide to the Architecture of Georgia

by

Tom Spector

Photography by
Susan Owings-Spector

University of South Carolina Press

Published in Columbia, South Carolina, by the
University of South Carolina Press

Manufactured in the United States of America

Library of Congress Cataloging-in-Publication Data

Spector, Tom, 1957–
    The guide to the architecture of Georgia / by Tom Spector ;
photography by Susan Owings-Spector.
        p. 175   cm.
    Includes bibliographical references and index.
    ISBN 0–87249–856–5
    1. Architecture—Georgia—Guidebooks. I. Owings-Spector, Susan.
    II. Title.
    NA730.G4S67   1993
    720' .9758—dc20   92–24631
                                                                        CIP

00001 4961

2. 13.93

Contents

Maps

Acknowledgments

This book has been made possible by those who have created, restored, and opened the featured works of architecture to the public. A sincere thanks to everyone who has taken to heart the cause of Georgia architecture. A few others have been helpful in the production of this work. Thanks to Fredda Swanson and Virginia Spector for their early proofreading; Billie Watson for additional fact checking and proofing; John Yau for advice and encouragement; John Linley, who told us it would take this long, but we did not believe him; and everyone at the University of South Carolina Press. My wife, Susan Owings-Spector, took the photographs and helped make this book possible through her support and companionship along every mile of the way.

How to Use This Book

This guide is designed as a resource for those who want to visit and enjoy the state's architecture. It is organized by region and further subdivided by county to allow the traveler to determine quickly what might be nearby to tour. Maps, photos, visiting information, and discussions accompany the entries. Essays are interspersed to help clarify important topics in Georgia's architectural heritage.

Many of the buildings listed are open to the public on some regular basis. However, their availability often depends on the efforts of a few dedicated individuals, so their status can change suddenly. Always call before planning a visit; an unanswered ring or disconnected line should be regarded as an ominous sign. While this book was being written, for instance, the wonderful Scarbrough House in Savannah was closed for restoration, then open to the public with regular visiting hours, then closed again. If buildings are described as private, then occupants should not be disturbed.

Accessibility for the handicapped varies widely for older buildings. An affirmation of accessibility usually guarantees only that the handicapped visitor can get to the front door and visit the main level. Commercial buildings constructed since the mid-1970s and government buildings have the highest levels of access for the handicapped. A building's accessibility often changes, too, so a call ahead might confirm improvements since this writing that now make a visit possible.

Buildings old enough to be considered historic are rarely in pristine shape. Conditions vary from just this side of collapse to gleaming. Most should be considered and appreciated as works in progress. Those that are fully restored are noted as such.

No encyclopedic, organized listing of Georgia's architectural resources exists, and it is not the purpose of this book to provide such a list. Inevitably I will have omitted someone's favorite building. For this I apologize in advance. While I have attempted to select those structures that give character to their regions and are truly worth the visit, the result is not a book that claims to have included every important building in this large state, but one that addresses the question "Now that I'm here, what can I see?"

The Guide to the Architecture of Georgia

Coastal Georgia

Savannah (Chatham County)

The Plan of Savannah

James Oglethorpe disembarked into the vast unfriendly wilderness called Georgia in 1733 fortified not with an army but with a town plan. Georgia's founding father understood a city's potential to influence society. The plan he had devised was to help him achieve his dream of establishing a colony where the indigent from England could flourish. It would provide standardized lots of sufficient size for decent housing, plenty of open space, identifiable neighborhoods, and places for public buildings. An easily extended pattern would accommodate expected growth. He named the town Savannah. Through Oglethorpe's visionary plan Georgia became the only state that began with an architectural concept.

What Oglethorpe initiated was nothing less than one of the most original urban designs executed in America. Washington, D.C., planned by Pierre-Charles L'Enfant, is made dramatic by its boulevards and diagonals; Savannah (whose plan predates L'Enfant's by seven decades) is made intimate and inviting by its pattern of well-defined squares. Each square defines the center of a ward (usually a group of four large blocks and four small blocks) and is pierced by a north-south street which lines up the centers of the squares. The major east-west streets do not go through the squares; they serve as boundaries for the wards.

While it is the squares that a visitor first perceives as distinctive about Savannah, these are simply the focus of a well-conceived hierarchy of spaces. Along the north and south sides of each square are the tything lots, those given or sold for personal residences. A sixty-foot by ninety-foot tything lot, a five-acre garden plot outside town, and a forty-four-acre farm in the country were given to each settler who came over with Oglethorpe in 1733. The tything lots were backed up by an alley. The smaller blocks on the east and west sides of the squares are called trust lots and were reserved for public buildings. To this day the smaller townhouses generally constitute the north and south sides of the squares while the public buildings, churches, and mansions occupy the trust lots. By following this plan each ward enjoys a mix of public and private buildings that distinguishes neighborhoods.

The squares had potential for defensive as well as aesthetic purpose. Since Savannah was a buffer colony against Spanish Florida, it had to be assumed that those working the farms might from time to time need to take refuge in the city. The squares could serve as overflow space for these refugees and their livestock.

During the eighteenth century the squares would have had an unkempt appearance. They were mostly surrounded by unpretentious wood houses and were not landscaped. Few buildings of this period survived the fire of 1796. The fire, however, coincided with the beginning of a new prosperity for Savannah as an important cotton shipping port. The new architecture was made of brick and was enriched with detailing of the Federal style. The nineteenth century saw the planting of the magnificent live oaks which give the squares much of their gentility. In the twentieth century the Historic Savannah Foundation has been the prime mover in bringing the older buildings back to their former grandeur and in creating the context in which the squares are probably more beautiful than ever before.

The triumph of the preservation movement in Savannah showcases the continued legitimacy of Oglethorpe's plan. Many towns that date from the Colonial period have been completely choked by automobile traffic. Savannah's fabric of alleys, streets, squares, and boulevards allows the city to continue to function ably within the confines of its 250-year-old plan. Though the sources for Oglethorpe's inspiration have been the subject for debate, his foresight has long been beyond question. Through this magnificent piece of urban design, James Oglethorpe became the first of many Georgians to understand and further the potential for architecture to enrich our lives.

For information contact:
Savannah Convention & Visitors Bureau, 301 West Broad Street, Savannah, GA 31402-1628, telephone: (912) 944-0456; Historic Savannah Foundation, P.O.Box 1733, Savannah, GA 31402, telephone: (912) 233-7787; or the Savannah Area Chamber of Commerce, 222 W. Oglethorpe, Savannah, GA 31401, telephone: (912) 944-0444.

ISAIAH DAVENPORT HOUSE (1)

324 E. State Street
Telephone: (912) 236-8097
Open Mon-Sat 10:00-4:30,
    Sun 1:30-4:30
Adults $4.00, children $3.00
Not handicapped accessible
Architect: Isaiah Davenport
Age: Built in 1821
Style: Federal

Isaiah Davenport House

14

This house, described in appreciative detail by Eugenia Price in her novel *Savannah*, is perhaps the most outstanding example of Federal style architecture in the city. The impending destruction of the Davenport house was the "cause célèbre" that led to the formation of the Historic Savannah Foundation. This house, with its four-over-four plan with a central hallway, is fully restored and decorated with period furnishings. The front hall is separated from the stair hall by a graceful archway on free-standing columns.

Nearby: WILLIAM KEHOE HOUSE (2), 123 Habersham Street (1893; DeWitt Bruyn, architect; private), is a stately three-story part Italianate and part Neoclassical home.

JAMES A. HABERSHAM JR. HOUSE (THE PINK HOUSE RESTAURANT) (3)

23 Abercorn Street. Telephone: (912) 232-4286
Open for lunch Mon-Sat 11:30-3:00, dinner 5:30-11:00
No admission fee
Architect: Unknown; remodeled by John S. Norris and others
Age: Built in 1789 with later additions

The Pink House is one of the few buildings left in Savannah from the eighteenth century. With its pink stucco exterior and dignified classical proportions, it is certainly the grandest. It has undergone several remodelings, and is now a restaurant.

CITY HALL (4)

Bay Street at Bull Street
Open Mon-Fri
9:00-5:00
No admission fee
Handicapped accessible
Architect: Hyman Witcover
Age: Built in 1905
Style: Neoclassical

The limestone City Hall facade is handsomely proportioned and topped by a stately domed tower that visually terminates Bull Street.

City Hall

15

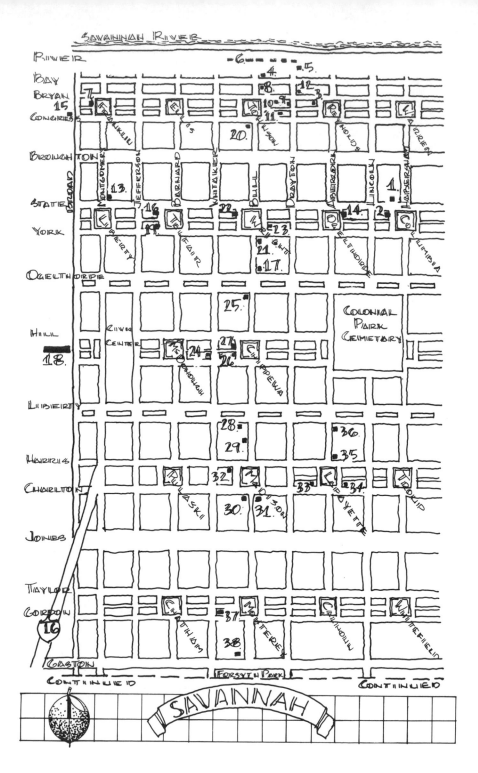

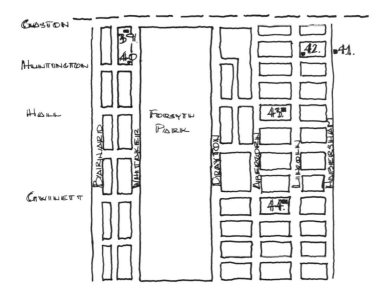

1. Isaiah Davenport House
2. Wm. Kehoe House
3. James A. Habersham Jr. House
4. City Hall
5. Savannah Cotton Exchange
6. Factors Walk & River Street
7. First African Baptist Church
8. U.S. Customs House
9. Citizens Bank
10. Savannah Bank & Trust
11. Christ Episcopal Church
12. Hibernia Bank
13. 116 Montgomery Street
14. Richard Richardson House
15. Scarbrough House
16. Telfair Academy Museum
17. Juliette Gordon Low House
18. Sav. Convention & Visitors Bur.
19. Trinity Methodist Church
20. Trust Co. Bank
21. 136 Bull Street
22. U.S. Post Office

23. Chatham Cty. Courthouse
24. Aaron Champion House
25. Ind. Presbyterian Church
26. 17 West McDonough
27. First Baptist Church
28. Francis Sorrell House
29. Georgia Hussars
30. Masonic Temple
31. Savannah Volunteer Guards
32. Green-Meldrim House
33. Andrew Low House
34. Samuel P. Hamilton House
35. Cathedral of St. John the Baptist
36. Sisters of Mercy Convent
37. Gen. Hugh Mercer House
38. Molyneux House
39. 501 Whitaker
40. 513 Whitaker
41. 402 E. Huntington
42. Meldrim Residence
43. Baldwin-Neely House
44. Hardee Residence

SAVANNAH COTTON EXCHANGE (5)

100 East Bay Street
Open Mon-Fri 9:00-5:00
No admission fee. Handicapped accessible
Architect: William G. Preston
Age: Built in 1886
Style: Romanesque Revival

Preston was Savannah's leading exponent of the Romanesque Revival style. He won a design competition for this commission. The stocky proportions of the pilasters and unusual use of the console motifs recall the work of Frank Furness in Philadelphia. Preston's terra cotta designs in the infill panels on the facade are extraordinarily rich.

Savannah Cotton Exchange

FACTORS WALK AND RIVER STREET (6)

Open all year as part of riverfront entertainment and shopping district
No admission fee. Handicapped accessible
Architect: Various builders
Age: Built ca.1850-1890
Style: Various

This long row of buildings along the Savannah River was ingeniously sited to make use of the steep bluff that fronts the water. The upper floors, accessible from the town side, were the offices of the cotton factors and shippers. The lower side, accessible from the river, was for warehousing. The catwalks from Bay Street to the offices served to allow the factors to inspect the cotton from above as it was brought in before it went down to the river to await export. Many of these buildings have been rehabilitated into offices, restaurants, and shops. The riverside has been landscaped and is now one of Savannah's prime tourist destinations.

Nearby: FIRST AFRICAN BAPTIST CHURCH (7), 23 Montgomery Street (1861), is open for services and special events. It features many ingenious Africa- inspired details.

U.S. CUSTOMS HOUSE (8)

1-5 East Bay Street (at Bull)
Open Mon-Fri 9:00-5:00
No admission fee
Architect: John S. Norris
Age: Built in 1848
Style: Neoclassical

The commission for this building brought New York architect John S. Norris to Savannah in what became a long and happy association between the city and the architect. The Customs House was the first in Savannah to be constructed with an iron framework. Norris proved to be a versatile designer in both types and styles of buildings. He is credited with institutional, church, mercantile, and residential buildings. His other works include his masterpiece in Savannah, the Gothic Revival style GREEN-MELDRIM HOUSE (32), the ANDREW LOW HOUSE (33), and the GENERAL HUGH MERCER HOUSE (37).

Nearby: CITIZENS BANK (9), 15 Drayton Street (1896; G. L. Norman, architect), is a five-story high-rise with a handsomely rusticated base.

SAVANNAH BANK & TRUST (10)

2-6 East Bryan Street
Open Mon-Fri 9:00-5:00
No admission fee
Architects: Mowbray & Uffinger
Age: Built in 1911
Style: Neoclassical

This building is a fourteen-story early skyscraper.

Nearby: CHRIST EPISCOPAL CHURCH **(11)**, 28 Bull Street (1838; James Hamilton Couper, architect). The interior was rebuilt in 1897.
HIBERNIA BANK **(12)**, 101 E. Bay Street (1912; Mowbray & Uffinger, architects) displays a severe Doric portico and is decidedly in the Greek style.
116 MONTGOMERY STREET **(13)**, (1916; Hyman Witcover, architect). The architect of City Hall also designed this heavily Moorish-influenced synagogue. The unadorned, arched entrance at the base contrasts markedly with highly ornate screens above, imparting an air of the exotic to this unusual building.

RICHARD RICHARDSON HOUSE (OWENS-THOMAS HOUSE & MUSEUM) (14)

124 Abercorn Street
Telephone: (912) 233-9743
Open Tues-Sat 10:00-5:00, Sun 2:00-5:00;
  closed September and major holidays
Adults $3.00, students $1.00
Architect: William Jay
Age: Built in 1818
Style: Regency

The residence for wealthy cotton merchant Richard Richardson was the commission which brought Mrs. Richardson's brother-in-law, the young English architect William Jay, to Savannah. After completing the Richardson commission, Jay went on to create a series of buildings that qualify as the state's first architectural masterpieces. Though several of Jay's buildings have been destroyed, this house and the two following this entry constitute an extraordinary part of Georgia's architectural heritage. They rank among the best works produced in America during this period. Sadly, Jay left Savannah and America before he was able to influence followers. His buildings stand isolated in the development of Georgia's architecture, having neither artistic predecessors nor successors.

Richard Richardson House

The sophisticated design of the Richardson house must have created quite a stir in what was then still basically a frontier town. Its plain surfaces, clean lines, and skillfully manipulated spaces were simply light years ahead of anything that had so far been produced in Georgia. The body of Jay's subsequent work in Savannah attests to the enthusiastic response this house received.

The distinctive feature on the front of the Richardson house is the delicately undulating portico. Jay's front porch is an oval space created by pulling the front of the porch forward and recessing the doorway. The elegant curved staircases leading to the street complete the composition.

The entrance hall is divided into two square volumes by the paired columns which create a separately defined stair hall. The switch-back stair is heavily proportioned and suitable for making grand entrances. The drawing room, with its rounded end wall and pendentive corner brackets, achieves a level of refinement still unsurpassed in the city.

At once grandiose and whimsical, the cast iron side porch is not to be missed. Its columns are supported by leafy consoles while the canopy is crested by antefixes. The seemingly weightless porch provides further evidence of Jay's rich talent.

SCARBROUGH HOUSE (15)

41 West Broad Street. Telephone: (912) 232-1177
Not open for regular tours, but has been in the past. Call the Telfair Academy for current status
Architect: William Jay
Age: Built in 1819
Style: Regency

The Scarbrough house, Jay's next commission after the Richardson House, is much more pared down, severe, and powerful. The Doric order portico gives weight and solemnity to the facade. This motif is echoed and exaggerated in the carriage gate to the right.

Inside, the central hall elaborates on the ideas introduced in the portico. This room is a two-story atrium-like space topped with a sky-blue vaulted ceiling lit by clerestory windows. The second-floor mezzanine is supported by Doric columns. The bold simplicity of this space has not been repeated in American domestic architecture.

Ionic order base molding, a Jay trademark, is used throughout the Scarbrough House. This type of tall base renders solidity to the walls and contrasts sharply with the light tracery crown moldings pulled free of the walls. Faux marble and faux wood grain painting are used on the base, columns, and paneling.

The stocky, masculine proportions of the house appear to be a comment on the more femininely ornamented Federal style houses that were the vogue at that time. Jay's spare detailing and modeling of space speak to a more modern sensibility.

21

Coastal Georgia

TELFAIR ACADEMY MUSEUM (TELFAIR HOUSE) (16)

Address: 121 Barnard Street. Telephone: (912) 232-1177
Open Tues-Sat 10:00-4:30, Sun 2:00-5:00
Adults $2.50, children $1.00. Handicapped accessible
Architect: William Jay
Age: Built in 1820; enlarged by Detlief Lienau in the 1880s
Style: Regency

William Jay's third residential project was the Telfair House (now the Telfair Academy Museum). This commission brought a return to a gentler expression of Jay's artistic explorations. The entrance hall repeats the wonderful atrium-like volume of the Scarbrough mansion but not its severity.

Strong geometries shape the salon rooms. The front left salon is a full octagon enlivened with a pattern of recesses and niches. The two large rooms towards the rear were both given full semicircular ends. This composition has been somewhat altered by the 1880s additions which turned the home into an art museum.

Telfair Academy Museum

JULIETTE GORDON LOW HOUSE & MUSEUM (JAMES MOORE WAYNE RESIDENCE) (17)

10 E. Oglethorpe Avenue. Telephone: (912) 233-4501
Open Mon, Tues, Thurs-Sat 10:00-4:00, Sun 11:00-4:30; closed Wed

Adults $3.00. Limited handicapped accessibility
Architect: Attributed to William Jay
Age: Built in 1820; remodeled and third floor added in 1886 by Detlief Lienau
Style: Regency

There is still some debate over whether or not Jay designed this house. In any event, Lienau's was an extensive reworking of the original house.

SAVANNAH CONVENTION & VISITORS BUREAU (18)

301 West Broad Street. Telephone: (912) 944-0456
Open Mon-Fri 8:30-5:00, Sat, Sun, and holidays 9:00-5:00
No admission fee. Handicapped accessible
Architect: Augustus Schwab
Age: Built in 1860
Style: Industrial

The former Central of Georgia Railway station is now a complete visitors center. This is a good first stop for newcomers to Savannah to gather information on the area and join tours.

Nearby: TRINITY METHODIST CHURCH (19) (1848; John B. Hogg, architect). This Greek Revival church displays a classically correct and handsome facade.

TRUST COMPANY BANK (20)

33 Bull Street on Johnson Square. Telephone: (912) 944-1000
Open Mon-Fri 9:00-5:00; closed holidays
No admission fee. Handicapped accessible
Architects: Cooper Carry & Associates
Style: Modern

Though it displaced several historic buildings, the Trust Company Bank shows how well a Modern building can fit into a historic setting without losing the feeling of its own time. Through judicious selection of materials, scaling, and rhythm of the openings this building complements its setting better than any other Modern building in town.

Nearby: 136 BULL STREET (21) (1890; Alfred Eichberg, architect). The first-floor facade of this four-story commercial building has many interesting details, but the entry on Bull Street, with its limestone columns and handsome iron gates, is particularly noteworthy.

U.S. POST OFFICE AND COURTHOUSE (22)

Wright Square, west side
Open Mon-Fri 9:00-5:00
No admission fee. Handicapped accessible
Architect: Jeremiah O'Rourke, with William Aiken as supervisory architect
Age: Built in 1895
Style: Italianate and Romanesque

The Post Office and Courthouse building expresses the solidity and gravity of the Romanesque but is lightened by a compatible Italianate flavor. The large, rough-hewn blocks of granite and round arches of the base are characteristic Romanesque elements. These motifs are echoed on the upper floors through bands of light-colored marble, arcaded loggias, and a distinctive tower. Such Italianate elements suggest the infuence of the famous Doges' Palace in Venice. The designers deserve high marks for having successfully scaled this massive block-long building appropriately to the surrounding structures.

U. S. Post Office and Courthouse

Nearby: CHATHAM COUNTY COURTHOUSE (23), 124 Bull Street (1889; William G. Preston, architect). The courthouse is Preston's largest commission in Savannah in the Romanesque Revival style.

AARON CHAMPION HOUSE (24)

230 Barnard Street
Not open to the public
Architect: Charles B. Cluskey
Age: Built in 1844; third floor added in 1895
Style: Greek Revival

Charles Cluskey was Georgia's premier architect during the period he practiced here, from 1830 to 1847. His commissions included the Medical College of Georgia in Augusta and the Old Governor's Mansion in Milledgeville. Born in Ireland and classically trained, Cluskey was one of the first designers to introduce the Greek Revival style into Georgia's residential architecture.

His work here reveals a progression toward the creation of his most accomplished Georgia building—the Old Governor's Mansion in Milledgeville. At the Champion House Cluskey began experimenting with the circular opening in the center hall which he would later develop into the rotunda. At this house he also introduced the spatial arrangement of a central back porch flanked by rear rooms, which became popular in Savannah. Other examples of Cluskey's work in Savannah are site numbers 26, 28, and 36.

INDEPENDENT PRESBYTERIAN CHURCH (25)

Bull Street at West Oglethorpe Street. Telephone: (912) 236-3346
Open during services
No admission fee
Architect: John Holden Greene
Age: Built in 1817; rebuilt by William G. Preston after a fire in 1891
Style: Neoclassical

John Holden Greene was the most famous architect practicing in Rhode Island at the time he took this commission. It is believed that Preston rebuilt the church following its original design. The steeple is particularly well conceived and is the tallest in the city.

Nearby: **17 WEST MCDONOUGH STREET (26)** (1844; attr. to Charles B. Cluskey, architect, third floor added in 1911; private). This grand Neoclassical house is unusual in that the imposing front porch is not the entry porch. The entry is on the side of the building.

FIRST BAPTIST CHURCH (27), 223 Bull Street (1833; Elias Carter, architect, 1922 remodeling by Henrik Wallin), is a correctly proportioned interpretation of a prostyle Greek temple.

FRANCIS SORRELL HOUSE (28), 6 West Harris Street (1841; Charles B. Cluskey, architect; private). This house appears to be Cluskey's interpretation of the William Jay houses in the city.

Coastal Georgia

The shop built for GEORGIA HUSSARS **(29)**, 307 Bull Street (1897), is one of Georgia's rare exotic revival buildings. This one is in the Moghul style.

MASONIC TEMPLE **(30)**, 321 Bull Street (1912; Hyman Witcover, architect), displays an unusual assembly of Classical elements.

SAVANNAH VOLUNTEER GUARDS **(31)**, 340 Bull Street (1893; William G. Preston, architect), is in the Romanesque revival style.

GREEN-MELDRIM HOUSE (32)

14 W. Macon Street, at Madison Square. Telephone: (912) 233-3845
Call for opening; this is the parish house of the Episcopal church next door
Architect: John S. Norris; restoration by W. Frank McCall
Age: Built in 1853
Style: Gothic Revival

Green-Meldrim House

This Norris masterpiece, which had the dubious honor of being General Sherman's headquarters when he arrived in Savannah, is one of Georgia's finest Gothic Revival buildings. Though the plan is a conventional four-over-four with a central hall, the detailing of the house establishes it as a break with the Classical styles of the first half of the century. The parapet and oriel windows are executed with medieval crenelations. A finely detailed iron porch extends around three sides of the house.

Inside, Gothic details are mixed with Classical elements. Niches and doorways are crowned with pointed arches, but heavy ceiling moldings of Gothic motif run continuously around the rooms in the Classical manner. The curving stair is light, elegant, and Classical in effect.

The Gothic in the Green-Meldrim House is elegant appliqué, not really integral to the design as it was to become in some of the churches of the period. The design is so charmingly executed, however, that the integrity of the scheme becomes only a secondary issue.

ANDREW LOW HOUSE (COLONIAL DAMES HOUSE) (33)

329 Abercorn Street. Telephone: (912) 233-6854
Open every day except Thurs 10:30-4:30; last tour begins at 4:00; closed holidays
Adults $2.00. Not handicapped accessible
Architect: Attributed to John S. Norris
Age: Built in 1849

This Italianate style house, the home of Girl Scouts founder Juliette Gordon Low from 1886 to 1927, has hosted Robert E. Lee and other important visitors. Its full restoration and furnishing in the Classical mode allow the visitor to see it as it looked when occupied by the Lows. The east facade is memorable for its elaborate cast iron work and the garden still retains its original design.

Nearby: SAMUEL P. HAMILTON HOUSE (34), 330 Abercorn Street (1873; J. D. Hall, architect; private). The Hamilton House is one of Savannah's few large homes executed in the Second Empire style, and it is in excellent condition.

CATHEDRAL OF ST. JOHN THE BAPTIST (35), Abercorn Street at East Harris Street (1872; Francis Baldwin, architect, rebuilt 1898). Open for services. This large church is a fully developed Gothic Revival design. It contains some excellent vaulting work and stained glass.

SISTERS OF MERCY CONVENT (36), 207 E. Liberty Street (not open to the public), is noteworthy primarily because it was designed by Charles B. Cluskey.

GENERAL HUGH W. MERCER HOUSE (37)

429 Bull Street
Private residence
Architects: John S. Norris; Muller & DeWitt Bruyn
Age: Built from 1860 to 1870
Style: Italianate

Designed on the eve of the Civil War, the Mercer house was not completed until a decade later by Norris's former assistants. By using fewer, larger windows, Norris achieved particularly handsome facades here. The house imparts a less repetitive, more open feeling than many Italianate buildings. Another novelty is the use of the first-floor window heads as balconies for the second-floor windows.

Nearby: MOLYNEUX HOUSE (38), 443-451 Bull Street (1917; Henrix Wallin, architect), is now a law office. This large house is a well executed Beaux-Arts design by one of Savannah's foremost early twentieth-century Classicists. It is connected to a garden pavilion by a gracefully curving colonnade.

VICTORIAN DISTRICT (39–44)

All buildings listed in the Victorian District are private homes except for 501 Whitaker. Many are opened from time to time during scheduled home tours. Contact Historic Savannah or the Savannah Convention & Visitors Bureau for more information.

501 WHITAKER (39) (1883; Detlief Lienau, architect). Home of Georgia Historical Society. Open Wed-Fri 10:00-5:00; no charge.

513 WHITAKER (40) (1903; G. L. Norman, architect). This home features an impressive semicircular Corinthian portico.

402 E. HUNTINGDON (41) (1892) is a charming and excessively ornate striped Queen Anne house.

TIEDMAN RESIDENCE (42) 226 E. Huntingdon (1890; Alfred Eichberg, architect). This heavy-looking brick structure shows evidence of a transition from late Victorian to Neoclassical detail.

BALDWIN-NEELY HOUSE (43) 225 E. Hall (1888; William G. Preston, architect). This is another extravaganza in brick by the architect of the Cotton Exchange. Almost every brick detail ever invented is incorporated somewhere. Turrets, arches, and bull's-eyes form a powerful play of circular geometries against a massive cubic form. Nos. 205, 208, and 213 on E. Hall Street are also worth seeing.

HARDEE RESIDENCE (44), 223 E. Gwinnett Street (1891; William G. Preston, architect), is a Queen Anne style home.

Brunswick (Glynn County)

For information contact:
Brunswick's Golden Isles of Georgia, Tourist and Convention Bureau, 4 Glynn
Avenue, Brunswick, GA 31521, telephone (912) 265-0620.

JEKYLL ISLAND CLUB (1)

Riverview Drive, Jekyll Island, GA 31520. Telephone: (912) 635-2600 or (800) 333-3333
Hotel is open all year
No admission fee
Architect: Charles Alexander; restoration by Larry Evans with interiors by Design Solutions
Age: Built in 1887; restored in 1987
Style: Eclectic, mostly Queen Anne

After decades of neglect, the Jekyll Island Club reopened in 1987 in mint
rehabilitated condition as a hotel run by the Radisson chain. The central hall and
the dining rooms combine elegant Classical detailing and rustic island construction for a successful effect.

MILLIONAIRES' HISTORIC DISTRICT (2-6)

Owned and operated by the State of Georgia
Jekyll Island, GA 31520. Telephone: (912) 635-2762 or Tourist Director
   (800) 342-1042 inside Georgia or (800) 841-6586 outside Georgia
Guided tours daily 10:00, 12:00, and 2:00; also a tour at 4:00 from Memorial
   Day to Labor Day
Adults $6.00, students $4.00. Handicapped accessible
Age: Built from 1890s to 1930
Style: Various

From the 1890s to the 1930s, Jekyll Island was a private retreat for wealthy
Northerners who came to escape the winter, hunt, and relax. Its decline came with
the ascendancy of south Florida as an accessible resort area. The millionaires left
behind some fine houses and what is now the rehabilitated JEKYLL ISLAND CLUB
(1).

There are several noteworthy structures on the tour:
INDIAN MOUND (2) (the Rockefeller cottage; 1892; Gordon Mackey, architect)
is a Shingle style home with three front parlors.
CRANE COTTAGE (3) (1916; David Adler, architect) is the most ostentatious
house on the island. It has a formal sunken garden with fountains and an arbor.

29

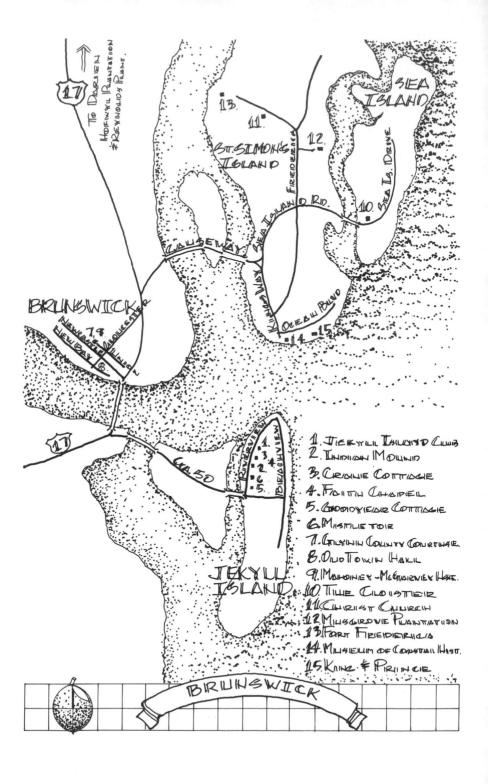

17

TO DARIEN
HOFWYL PLANTATION
& REYNOLDS PLANTATION

SEA
ISLAND

13.
11.
ST. SIMON'S
ISLAND
12.

SEA IS. DRIVE

FRIEDERICA

10.

SEA ISLAND RD.

CAUSEWAY

SEA ISLAND

BRUNSWICK
GLOUCESTER

NEWCASTLE

NEWCASTLE
7.
HILLTON

NEW BAY 8.

KINGS WAY

OCEAN BLVD

14. 15.

17

GA. 50

RIVERVIEW
BEACHVIEW

1.
3.
4.
2.
6.
5.

JEKYLL
ISLAND

1. JEKYLL ISLAND CLUB
2. INDIAN MOUND
3. CRANE COTTAGE
4. FAITH CHAPEL
5. GOODYEAR COTTAGE
6. MISTLETOE
7. GLYNN COUNTY COURTHSE.
8. OLD TOWN HALL
9. MAHONEY-McGARVEY HSE.
10. THE CLOISTER
11. CHRIST CHURCH
12. MUSGROVE PLANTATION
13. FORT FREDERICA
14. MUSEUM OF COASTAL HIST.
15. KING & PRINCE

BRUNSWICK

FAITH CHAPEL (4) (1904) is a small rustic Gothic Revival style building. The stained glass behind the pulpit is by Maitland Armstrong; the front window illustrating the Old Testament is signed by Louis Comfort Tiffany.

GOODYEAR COTTAGE (5) (1907) was designed by Hastings & Carrere, the architects for the New York Public Library. It is now home to the Jekyll Island Art Association.

MISTLETOE (6) (1907; Charles Allen Gifford, architect) is a Shingle style cottage designed for Henry Allen Porter.

Indian Mound

GLYNN COUNTY COURTHOUSE (7)

Courthouse Square, Union Street at G Street, Brunswick
Open Mon-Fri 9:00-5:00
No admission fee. Handicapped accessible
Architects: C. A. Gifford & E. S. Betts
Age: Built in 1907
Style: Neoclassical

This is the loveliest courthouse in Georgia. The stately Neoclassical building is set in the middle of a square lushly landscaped with palm trees, giant azaleas, and moss-hung live oaks.

Nearby: OLD TOWN HALL (8), Queens Square. This building, which serves as the home of the Preservation Society, has a heroic arched entrance flanked by turrets.

The MAHONY-McGARVEY HOUSE (9), west side of Courthouse Square (private), is an 1891 Queen Anne extravaganza.

10 miles north of Brunswick on U.S. 17 is the HOFWYL PLANTATION HISTORIC SITE (not on map), operated by the Georgia Department of Natural Resources (Route 2, Box 83, Brunswick, GA 31520; telephone (912) 264-9263).

The town of Darien (20 miles north of Brunswick) is the place from which to leave for a visit to Sapelo Island and the REYNOLDS PLANTATION (not on map). Saturday bus tours arranged through the Chamber of Commerce include the island and the grounds of the fourteen-bedroom house (interiors are not open). Darien Chamber of Commerce, P.O. Box 1497, Darien, GA 31305; telephone (912) 437-4192.

The Cloister

THE CLOISTER (10)

Sea Island, GA 31561. Telephone: (912) 638-3611
Open all year.
No admission fee. Handicapped accessible
Architect: Addison Mizner
Age: Built in 1928
Style: Spanish Revival

The Cloister opened as Georgia's finest resort hotel in 1928 amid much fanfare and with trainloads of dignitaries. It has retained that status to this day. The design, by famous Palm Beach architect Addison Mizner, is a surprisingly restrained rendition of the Spanish style he developed for the ritzy Florida resort.

Restraint is the watchword for the interiors as well as for the facades. Though rich in detail and spatial ingenuity, the public rooms never lapse into opulence. Heavy beamwork and massive rectangular piers—a theme repeated in most public rooms—give order and character to the composition. The most ornate room, the Spanish Lounge, retains many of the original Mizner-designed furnishings.

The building's rambling, informal layout has accommodated additions gracefully over the years. Today's Cloister is a huge complex of guest villas, activities buildings, and hotel annexes. Although these additions do not extend the spatial ingenuity of the original building, they do fit attractively in the subtropical landscape of Sea Island. The Cloister stands at the entry to an island literally chock-full of dream house villas easily enjoyed on a driving tour. The most famous of these is influential architect John Portman's exuberant resort home (private) on 26th Street.

CHRIST CHURCH (11)

Frederica Road, P.O. Box 1185, Saint Simons Island, GA 31522
Telephone: (912) 638-8683
Open daily 2.00-5.00 in the summer, 1:00-4:00 in the winter, and for church services
No admission fee, although a donation is appreciated. Handicapped accessible
Age: Built in 1884
Style: Gothic Revival

At the northern end of Saint Simons Island, Christ Church was erected in 1884 on the site of an original 1820s church burned during the Civil War. The gleaming white lapped-siding building stands out brilliantly against the green canopy of live oaks and the emerald lawn. As you enter the walled churchyard through a handsome entry arch, a garden pathway leads to the entrance in the base of the tower. The natural wood interior displays a roof frame carefully fitted together by the two ship's carpenters who were its builders.

Christ Church

MUSGROVE PLANTATION (12)

Frederica Road, Saint Simons Island
Private, but frequently open during the annual Tour of Homes and Gardens, sponsored by the
    Episcopal Churchwomen of Christ Church, Frederica, held in late March.
Admission fee: Must buy tour ticket. For further information contact Christ Church, Frederica,
    P.O. Box 1185, Saint Simons Island, GA 31522; telephone (912) 638-8638
Architect: Francis Abreu

This 400+ acre private estate at the edge of the marsh is open to the public most years during the annual Tour of Homes and Gardens. If it is not formally open, do not try to visit it; if it is open, don't miss it. Musgrove Plantation is to other resort homes what Chartres is to cathedrals.

The long driveway to the house is an essay in the use of coastal vegetation to create drama and expectation. Twisting wisteria vines drape across the roadway. Palmettos close in on the roadsides, then suddenly give way to groves of cedars and live oaks. A bridge over a reed-lined pond marks the final approach to the main house.

The entry facade of the house deflates any expectations of grandeur; it seems rustic and small. Actually its mass is deliberately broken up to keep it more in scale with the natural surroundings. Its weathered appearance is also a cultivated effect.

34

Clay roof tiles are formed to look like shakes, and the heart cypress siding was painted when wet so that it would mildew prematurely.

A small entry vestibule opens onto the two-story living room terminated by a large bowed window wall overlooking the formal garden and marshes. Opposite the window wall is a walk-in fireplace and mezzanine. Flanking the room are identical recreation rooms, which in turn are terminated by bowed walls. Materials inside are tabby, terrazzo, and bleached wood, the last used in beams and trusses. The exposed truss design recalls that of Christ Church.

The bowed walls and elliptical peak window introduce the elliptical geometry so effectively used by landscape architect T. M. Baumgardner in the gardens on the marsh side. This geometric theme, carried into the design of the pool, trellis, and formal garden, contrasts sharply with the untamed marshes so close by.

Musgrove Plantation

Nearby: FORT FREDERICA NATIONAL MONUMENT (13), Frederica Road; telephone (912) 638-3639. Once a thriving colonial outpost, Fort Frederica burned in 1758 after having been an important deterrent against the Spanish during the War of Jenkins' Ear. Its interest now is primarily archaeological. Open daily 8:00-5:00; donation accepted.

One of only two Georgia lighthouses has been incorporated into the MUSEUM OF COASTAL HISTORY (14) (1872). The lighthouse, a conical stucco structure, offers from its top the best available view of the surrounding area. The adjacent Museum of Coastal History is the lighthouse caretaker's well-preserved Federal style cottage. Open Tues-Sat 10:00-5:00, Sun 1:30-5:00; Adults $2.00, children free.

THE KING & PRINCE HOTEL (15) is a sensitive rehabilitation (1985; Fullerton & Associates, architects, Miami) of the old resort hotel originally built in 1935 as the Jewish alternative to The Cloister. The dining room has some excellent stained glass panels original to the hotel by High Point Glass of North Carolina. Telephone (800) 342-0212 or (912) 638-3631.

Cumberland Island and Saint Marys (Camden County)

Lovely and seemingly forgotten by coastal development, Saint Marys is the place to catch the ferry to Cumberland Island. The town is easily visited on a walking tour down Osborne Street to the river. The historic buildings are well marked along the way.

Cumberland Island, accessible only by ferry, has been inhabited for hundreds of years, and Indian settlements are known to have been on the Plum Orchard site. In the 1700s and 1800s islanders developed cotton and indigo plantations. In the late 1800s Thomas Carnegie began buying island real estate and continued until he owned about ninety percent of the land.

Now ninety percent of the island is controlled by the National Park Service. Notable exceptions are the Greyfield Inn, owned by Carnegie descendants, and the Northern tip of the island, which is owned by the Candler family. Approximately 40 people live on the sixteen-mile-long island, and the Park Service limits visitors to about 300 at any given time. As a result of limited development and access, Cumberland Island has preserved some of the most hauntingly beautiful beaches in the nation.

For information contact:
Cumberland Island National Seashore, P.O. Box 806, Saint Marys, GA 31558.

PLUM ORCHARD MANSION (1)

Plum Orchard Historic District, Cumberland Island, P.O. Box 806, Saint Marys, GA 31558
Telephone: (912) 882-4335
Open by guided tour only on Sunday afternoons, April-September, and the first Sunday of the month, October-March. Reservations are recommended

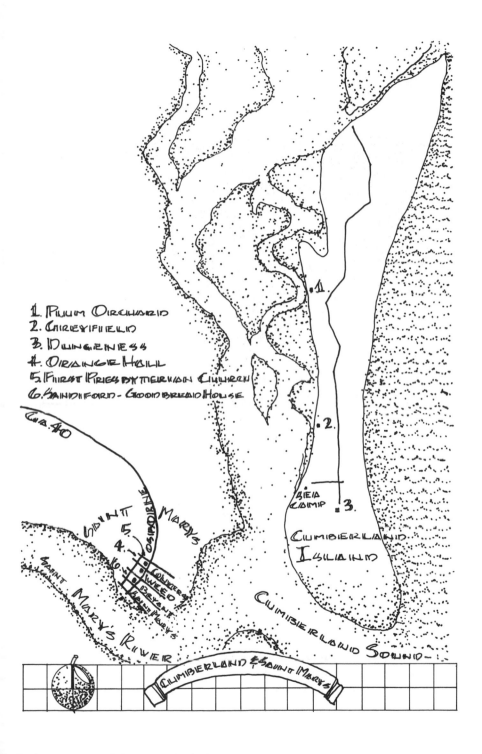

1. PLUM ORCHARD
2. CHIREYIFIELD
3. DUNGENESS
4. ORANGE HILL
5. FIRST PRESBYTERIAN CHURCH
6. SANDIFORD - GOODBREAD HOUSE

CTR. 40

SAINT MARYS
OSBORNE

5
4
6
OLIVER
TWEED
SAINT MARYS

SAINT MARYS RIVER

SAINT MARYS

•1

•2

SEA
CAMP
•3

CUMBERLAND
ISLAND

CUMBERLAND SOUND

CUMBERLAND SOUND—

CUMBERLAND & SAINT MARYS

Coastal Georgia

Tour departs Saint Marys at 11:45. Admission is $6.00 plus ferry fee
Only the first floor of Plum Orchard is handicapped accessible
Architects: Peabody & Stern, Boston
Age: Built in 1898 with later additions

Plum Orchard

Built for George and Margaret Carnegie, Plum Orchard was the second grandest of the Carnegie mansions on Cumberland Island. The house eventually encompassed thirty rooms as well as an indoor pool and squash courts. Its extensive grounds included tennis courts, polo fields, gardens, and a duck pond.

The exterior is a formal Neoclassical composition in stucco. A grand Roman portico leads to a less forbidding interior that relies more on superb woodwork than on elaborate moldings for its refinements. The game room, with its Tiffany tortoise-shell-motif lamps, and the entry hall stair and fireplace composition are highlights of the tour.

Plum Orchard is run today on a meager National Park Service budget. Donations for restoration work are requested at the end of the tour.

Nearby: **GREYFIELD (2)** (1902; MacClure & Spahr, Pittsburgh, architects) was built for Margaret Carnegie as a wedding present. Informal yet imposing, Greyfield is a three-story-plus-attic home with the living spaces and porch on a raised first floor. Its style springs from the Early American Revival tradition. Greyfield appears to be a Northern architect's interpretation of a Southern plantation home. The house, now called the Greyfield Inn, is managed by a Carnegie descendant. Reservations are required. Contact Greyfield Inn, Drawer B, Fernandina Beach, FL 32034; telephone: (904) 261-6408.

DUNGENESS (3)

Cumberland Island, GA 31558
Telephone: National Park Service (912) 882-4335
Open all year, but reservations are needed to visit the island
No admission fee. Handicapped accessible
Architects: Peabody & Stern, Boston
Age: Built in 1885

Dungeness

On the Southern tip of Cumberland Island stands the state's most magnificent ruin; the romantic vine-covered skeleton of Thomas and Lucy Carnegie's mansion, Dungeness. It superseded an earlier, much plainer Dungeness built by Revolutionary War hero General Nathanael Greene. The home was a massive mansion in the Newport, Rhode Island, style. Arson was apparently the cause of its destruction in 1959. The National Park Service has thoroughly documented the estate and makes available several displays and tours.

ORANGE HALL (4)

Osborne Street at Conyers Street, Saint Marys
Telephone: (912) 882-4000
Open Mon-Sat 9:00-12:00 and 1:00-5:00, Sun 1:00-5:00
Adults $2.00. Not handicapped accessible
Age: Built in 1820s

Orange Hall is a four-over-four house placed entirely (and quite sensibly, given the climate) on a raised basement. The elevated front porch and living rooms are positioned to take maximum advantage of any coastal breezes and to elevate the residents above the worst of the insect problem. It is now a house museum and welcome center.

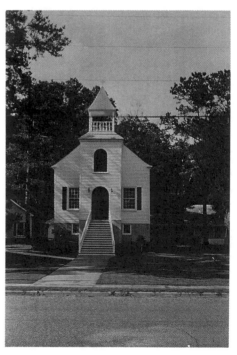

Nearby: Across the street, the chapel of the FIRST PRESBYTE-RIAN CHURCH (5) (1822), the oldest Presbyterian church in the state, is also elevated. The staircase successfully shortens the perspective by narrowing as it ascends to the front porch and belfry. The result is a little church that is imposing beyond its size.

One of the most fetching homes on Osborne Street is the SANDIFORD-GOODBREAD HOUSE (6) (c. 1885). It is a two-story cottage restored and now used as an inn. Telephone: (912) 882-7490.

First Presbyterian Church

South Central and Southwest Georgia

Valdosta (Lowndes County)

Valdosta became the county seat when the old Lowndes County Courthouse at Troupville burned and the citizens elected to build the new one on a site along the railroad line. This brought a period of prosperity to Valdosta, which quickly became south central Georgia's administrative and distribution center. The town was at the forefront of the general prosperity Georgia experienced in the late 1800s as a center for the production of both Sea Island cotton and forest products.

Valdosta's finest structures date from the 1890s through the second decade of the 1900s when the boll weevil brought destruction to Georgia's cotton industry. The city is organized for the most part on a north-south spine. The preeminent street for architecture is Patterson Street, which meets its important cross axis, Central Street, at Courthouse Square. An active redevelopment effort has spurred a general rehabilitation of the mercantile structures in the seven blocks that comprise the core of Valdosta's downtown.

Three of the finest turn-of-the-century residences in the downtown area have been successfully rehabilitated for public uses. These are THE CRESCENT (1), presently the home to the Valdosta garden clubs; the BARBER HOUSE (2), serving as headquarters for the Chamber of Commerce; and the CONVERSE-DALTON HOUSE (3), now home to the Junior Service League.

For information contact:
Chamber of Commerce, P.O. Box 790, Valdosta, GA 31603-0790.

THE CRESCENT (SENATOR W. S. WEST HOUSE) (1)

904 N. Patterson Street
Open Mon-Fri 2:00-5:00; also during Heritage Foundation spring tour,
   first weekend in December, and for special functions.
No admission fee. Not handicapped accessible
Architects: Beckly & Tyler, Atlanta
Age: Built in 1889
Style: Neoclassical

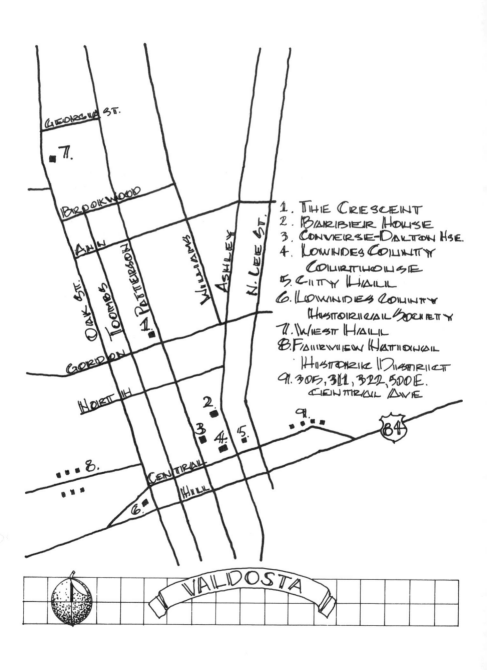

GEORGIA ST.

7.

BROOKWOOD

ANN

OAK ST.

TOOMBS

PATTERSON

WILLIAMS

ASHLEY

N. LEE ST.

1. THE CRESCENT
2. BARBER HOUSE
3. CONVERSE-DALTON HSE.
4. LOWNDES COUNTY
   COURTHOUSE
5. CITY HALL
6. LOWNDES COUNTY
   HISTORICAL SOCIETY
7. WEST HALL
8. FAIRVIEW NATIONAL
   HISTORIC DISTRICT
9. 305, 311, 322, 500 E.
   CENTRAL AVE

GORDON

NORTH

2.

9.

3. 4. 5.

84

8.

CENTRAL

HILL

6.

VALDOSTA

The Crescent

Valdosta's grandest residential structure, The Crescent flaunts what is probably the most impressive colonnade on any house in the state. Fifteen huge Ionic columns support a massive curved entablature that encircles three sides of the house. Under the portico a curved balcony surmounts a Palladian entry.

Inside, the side walls of the entry hall are placed at 45-degree angles to the front door, creating an interesting triangular space. This triangular geometry meets the long cross axis of the hallway and is well resolved in the imaginative beamwork and ceiling moldings. To the rear of the entry hall a grand stair hall creates a lively two-story volume with balconies on three sides. Nearly all the second-story rooms open off this central space.

Partially revealed from the entry hall above and behind the stair hall is the much smaller stair up to the third-floor ballroom. The ballroom is a wide, sweeping space spanning the entire length of the house. It contains an alcove in the center of one of the long walls for an orchestra. The alcove is flanked by lounges for ladies and gentlemen who wished to relax away from the main activity.

Several rooms on the first floor exhibit great spatial variety and character. The library and men's parlor on either side of the entry hall are seven-sided. The ladies' parlor is L-shaped. One end of the dining room terminates in a semicircular solarium. The rooms are furnished throughout with turn-of-the-century pieces, many original to the house. The chaperon sofa upstairs is a particularly unusual piece.

The Valdosta garden clubs maintain the structure in mint condition and have added a formal garden with a fountain in the rear. Recently brought to the grounds is an octagonal building built in 1913 for a progressive kindergarten. The Octagon style never found much favor in Georgia. This is a rare, albeit late, example and one of only two in the state available for public view.

BARBER HOUSE (2)

Chamber of Commerce, 416 N. Ashley Street, P.O. Box 790, Valdosta, GA 31603-0790. Telephone: (912) 247-8100
Open Mon-Fri 9:00-5:00
No Admission fee. Not handicapped accessible
Architect: Lloyd Barton Greer; 1980 renovation consultant, W. Frank McCall
Age: Built in 1915
Style: Neoclassical

Barber House

The Barber House is a fine example of a Neoclassical residence brought back to life in a sensitive rehabilitation. An Ionic front porch supports a bracketed overhanging cornice revealing elements of the Italianate style, which would have been receding in favor by the time of this house's construction.

Under the portico a partially recessed balcony hangs over the fanlight-topped entry. The central hall is two rooms deep with the stair tucked behind the first room. Unique original brass light fixtures have been repaired, and more than 50 pieces of furniture original to the house have been retained. Upholstery, wallcoverings, and colors have been chosen to replicate those of the period when the house was constructed.

CONVERSE-DALTON HOUSE (3)

305 N. Patterson Street. Telephone: (912) 244-8574
Open Fri 2:00-5:00
No admission fee. Not handicapped accessible
Architect: Unknown
Age: Built in 1902
Style: Queen Anne and Greek Revival

This residential structure is a hybrid of Queen Anne massing surrounded by a Greek Revival portico. The unusual, slenderly proportioned Composite-order

44

columns on stone piers support a completely unacademic entablature that contains two rows of dentils and is topped by an Italianate bracketed eave. The ornately carved wood balcony over the entry is visually supported by elaborate brackets on Composite-order columns. The composition artfully frames the double doors and mediates between the scale of the portico columns and the doorway. Inside the entry hall a grand stair is oriented perpendicularly to the axis of the main hall through the house. The Converse-Dalton House is now the home of the Valdosta Junior League.

LOWNDES COUNTY COURTHOUSE (4)

> Patterson Street at Central Avenue
> Open Mon-Fri 9:00-5:00
> No admission fee. Handicapped accessible
> Architect: Frank P. Milburn; restored in 1986 by Art Smith
> Age: Built in 1904
> Style: Neoclassical

This three-story structure has an impressive central cupola-topped dome as well as a dome at each corner. The recent restoration brought back the original detail and impressive cubic volume of the second-floor courtroom.

VALDOSTA CITY HALL (5)

> Central Avenue at N. Lee Street
> Open Mon-Fri 9:00-5:00
> No admission fee
> Handicapped accessible
> Architect: Lloyd Greer
> Age: Built in1910
> Style: Neoclassical

Valdosta City Hall

This former U.S. Courthouse and Post Office contains extensive plasterwork rendering of beams, egg and dart molding, and oak leaves on the first floor. A handsome cast iron staircase leads up to the second-floor courtroom now used as a city council meeting room.

Nearby: LOWNDES COUNTY HISTORICAL SOCIETY AND MUSEUM (6), 305 W. Central Avenue (Lloyd Greer, architect), was formerly the Carnegie Library. Open Sun 3:00-5:00.

WEST HALL, VALDOSTA STATE COLLEGE (7), N. Patterson Street at Georgia

Avenue (Blake Ellis, architect), is the administration building of Valdosta State College. The Spanish Colonial Revival building has a smooth stucco exterior and tiled roofs. A shallow dome and cupola focus attention toward the center of the facade and the arched entry. Telephone: (912) 333-5952; open Mon-Fri 9:00-5:00; closed during college vacations.

The FAIRVIEW NATIONAL HISTORIC DISTRICT (8), clustering around River and Wells Streets, has some impressive Victorian-era homes in various stages of restoration or neglect. Other Victorian period homes (private) are located at **305, 311, 322,** and **500 E. CENTRAL AVENUE (9).**

Thomasville (Thomas and Grady Counties)

For information contact:
Chamber of Commerce Welcome Center, 401 S. Broad Street, Thomasville, GA 31799, telephone (912) 226-9600.

LAPHAM-PATTERSON HOUSE (1)

> 626 Dawson Street. Telephone: (912) 226-0405
> Open Tues-Sat 9:00-5:00, Sun 2:00-5:30; closed Thanksgiving and Christmas
> Adults $1.00. Partially handicapped accessible
> Architect: Attributed to T. J. P. Rommerdall
> Age: Built in 1884-1885
> Style: Mixed Victorian era styles

One of Georgia's most idiosyncratic houses, The Lapham-Patterson house is thought to be the first work of Chicago architect-contractor T. J. P. Rommerdall. Rommerdall, killed in a construction accident in Thomasville, left a small body of work here that included an Octagonal house and the Masbury Hotel. Neither had the exuberance and bravado of the winter home of C. W. Lapham.

As though the house were a product of a mystical fear of repetition, no two rooms have the same shape, and none are rectangular. This Victorian mishmash is somehow given an organized form on the exterior, which is detailed in Queen Anne and Eastlake motifs.

The carefree informality of the facades gives way to a deliberate quirkiness inside that varies from playful to unsettling. The strange geometries of the rooms are at times beautifully resolved in the wood flooring patterns and at other times blithely ignored.

The staircase is the tour de force of the interior. The chimney of the large dining room fireplace is split and penetrated by the main stair, which rises from behind

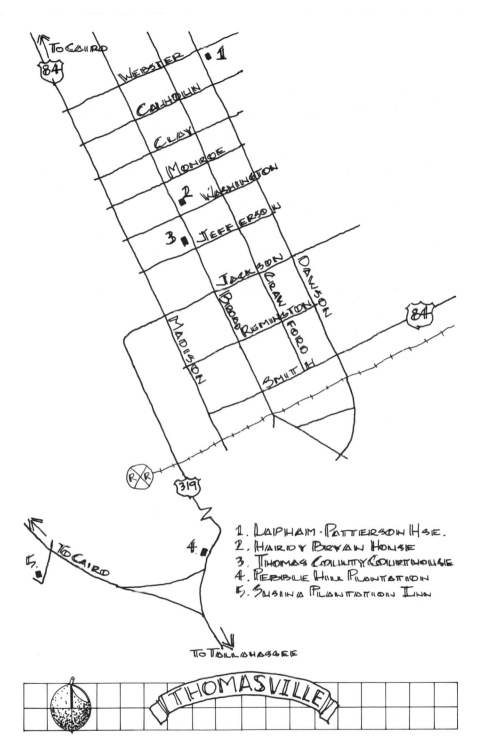

To Cairo
84

Webster
• 1
Calhoun
Clay
Monroe
2 Washington
Jefferson
3
Jackson
Dawson
Crawford
Madison
Pinto
Remington
84
Smith

R R
319

To Cairo
4.
5.

1. Lapham-Patterson Hse.
2. Hardy Bryan House
3. Thomas County Courthouse
4. Pebble Hill Plantation
5. Susina Plantation Inn

To Tallahassee

THOMASVILLE

Lapham-Patterson House

the fireplace to a cantilevered landing on the front side. The landing, which at first glance appears to be an incredibly overscaled mantle, leads to the second flight of stairs, which disappears in an abrupt left turn before reaching the second floor. Odd but engaging, this design is evidence of a talent unafraid to challenge conventional ideas of space-making. The incorporation into the house of the latest gas lighting, indoor plumbing, and modern closets provides further proof of Rommerdall's forward thinking. The Lapham-Patterson house leaves the viewer wondering what further challenges Rommerdall's work would have presented had his career not been cut so tragically short.

Nearby: Also in the downtown area is the HARDY BRYAN HOUSE (2), 312 N. Broad Street (restoration by W. Frank McCall, architect). Telephone (912) 226-6016 for opening times. Built in 1833, it is now the home of Thomasville Landmarks Inc. This square-columned house is thought to be Thomasville's oldest two-story home and the precursor to all of Thomas County's Greek Revival plantations.

The THOMAS COUNTY COURTHOUSE (3) (1858; John Wind, architect), on Broad between Jefferson and Washington, is one of the state's oldest courthouses.

PEBBLE HILL PLANTATION (4)

South of Thomasville on US 319, P.O. Box 830, Thomasville, GA 31799
Telephone: (912) 226-2344

Thomasville (Thomas and Grady Counties)

Open Tues-Sat 10:00-5:00, Sun 1:00-5:00 (last tour begins at 4:00); closed Labor Day to
October 1, Thanksgiving, and Christmas
Admission to grounds only, adults $2.00, children $1.00; house
museum: $5.00 (children under 12 not admitted to house)
Architect: Abram Garfield, Cleveland
Age: Built in 1936
Style: Neoclassical with Jeffersonian-inspired design

Pebble Hill is one of dozens of "plantations" between Thomasville and
Tallahassee that existed primarily as winter retreats for Northern families (particularly families from Cleveland). Like most of these plantations, Pebble Hill was
engaged in very little farming. It was maintained primarily for recreation and
hunting. The undergrowth in the tall pine forests is regularly burned off to create
the optimum quail hunting environment.

The original Pebble Hill house, built in 1850 and attributed to local architect
John Wind, burned in the 1930s. The bulk of the present-day mansion dates from
1936. The house, stables, and gate house are all by Garfield; the latter two
buildings are designed with a pronounced Jeffersonian flavor. Though basically
Neoclassical, the structure displays some distinct Greek Revival and rustic
touches on the exterior.

The interior contains a collection of furnished rooms in a good state of
preservation. Particularly noteworthy are the dining room, with its faux marble
columns and panels; the cupola-topped staircase; and the long, sunny gallery. The
interior can be seen only on a ninety-minute tour.

SUSINA PLANTATION INN (5)

Route 3, Box 1010,
Thomasville, GA 31792. 4
miles west of US 319 on the
Meridian Road (GA 155) in
Grady County. Telephone:
(912) 377-9644
Open as an inn and restaurant.
Dinner to nonregistered guests
by reservation only. An arts
and crafts fair is hosted here
in early March
No admission fee
Architects: John Wind & T.
Blackshear
Age: Built c. 1841
Style: Greek Revival

Susina Plantation Inn

This authentic Greek Revival Plantation house displays an impressive Ionic portico and contains an elegant curved staircase and well-decorated public rooms. The side porches and rear extension are 1890s additions.

Bainbridge (Decatur County)

The fine old houses on Shotwell Street and surrounding streets are reminders of Bainbridge's heyday as the center of a booming lumber industry. Queen Anne and Neoclassical styles predominate. Home tours are held at irregular intervals and are sponsored by the Junior Women's Club and the Bainbridge Historical Society.

For information contact:
Chamber of Commerce, P.O. Box 736, Bainbridge, GA 31717, telephone (912) 246-4774.

FIRST UNITED METHODIST CHURCH (1)

> Shotwell Street at Florida Street. Telephone:
> (912) 246-1864
> Open for worship and during office hours
> No admission fee
> Limited handicapped accessibility
> Architect: W. B. Camp, Jacksonville
> Age: Built in 1911
> Style: Mixed

First United Methodist Church

The semicircular chapel design used in this church was popular in Bainbridge. This building also features large, arched stained-glass windows on three sides.

Nearby: DECATUR COUNTY COURTHOUSE (2), West Street at Water Street (1902; Alexander Blair, architect), is in the Neoclassical style rather than in the more common Romanesque style so popular in Georgia courthouses of the period. It features an impressive Corinthian porch and an even more impressive six-story tower.

ST. JOHN'S EPISCOPAL CHURCH (3), Broughton Street at Hall Street, is an excellent example of the spare, unpretentious gracefulness that could be achieved in the Carpenter Gothic style. The pews and windows are original to the building.

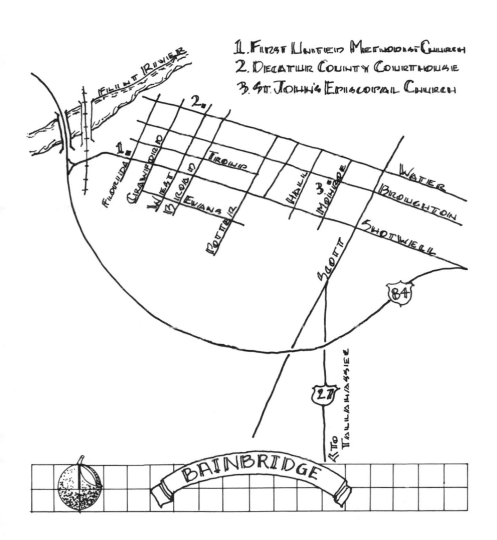

1. FIRST UNITED METHODIST CHURCH
2. DECATUR COUNTY COURTHOUSE
3. ST. JOHN'S EPISCOPAL CHURCH

FLINT RIVER

FLORIDA
CRAWFORD RD
WEST
BROAD RD
TROUP
EVANS
POTTER
HALL
MOORE
WATER
BROUGHTON
SHOTWELL
SCOTT
84
27
TO TALLAHASSEE

BAINBRIDGE

Albany (Dougherty County)

Albany's status as the center of the state's important pecan industry has had a salutary effect on the surrounding landscape. The pecan tree's massive, pier-like trunks support arching branches of such span that entire homes can be built between rows without disturbing a single tree. The well-ordered groves create inviting, dappled-shade arcades that stretch to the horizon and give the effect of a natural architecture of cathedral-like proportions lining the roads to this town.

Albany's significant offerings of art and entertainment are evidence of a community with long suits in pride and spirit. These obvious strengths seem at odds with the antiurban impression resulting from the wrecking ball's effect on the downtown. Some impressive older buildings remain, however, such as the CHAMBER OF COMMERCE (1), WILLIAM SMITH HOUSE (3), AND ALBANY LITTLE THEATER (4).

For information contact:
Albany Chamber of Commerce and Convention & Visitors Bureau, P.O. Box 308,
Albany, GA 31702.

ALBANY CHAMBER OF COMMERCE (OLD FIRST STATE BANK BUILDING) (1)

225 W. Broad Street, Albany, GA 31702
Telephone: (912) 434-8700
Open Mon-Fri 9:00-5:00
No admission fee
Handicapped accessible
Architect: Rehabilitation by Buckley & Associates
Age: Built in 1928, remodeled in 1989

The Chamber of Commerce is housed in a temple-like former bank building in the center of town. The sensitively rehabilitated building

Albany Chamber of Commerce

maintains its dignity despite being the only older building in a block otherwise slated for urban renewal into a downtown plaza.

Nearby: Several significant buildings, all in Neoclassical expressions, ring the future plaza. Most impressive of these is the MUNICIPAL AUDITORIUM (2), Pine Street at Jackson Street, which fairly sparkles from its 1989 restoration. Open for performances; handicapped accessible.

WILLIAM SMITH HOUSE (3), 516 Flint Street, is the oldest brick structure in Albany (1860). It is well tended by the local Junior League. A classic two-over-

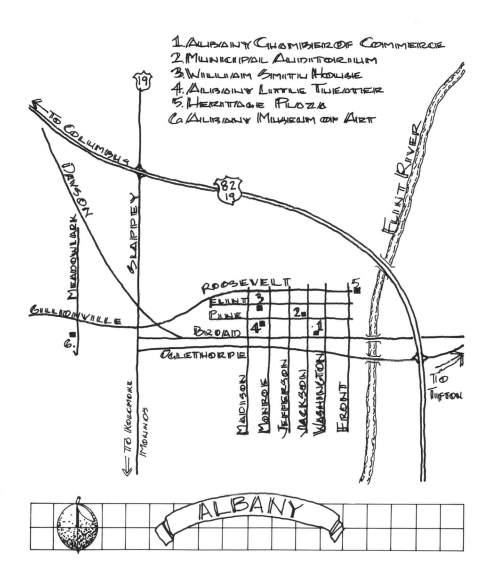

1. Albany Chamber of Commerce
2. Municipal Auditorium
3. William Smith House
4. Albany Little Theater
5. Heritage Plaza
6. Albany Museum of Art

ALBANY

two plan, the house contains a handsome semicircular mahogany staircase and reestablished parterre gardens. You may be allowed in if you can catch someone in the office in back.

Also nearby, at 514 Pine, the ALBANY LITTLE THEATER (4) performs its impressive yearly repertoire in the enlarged Captain John A. Davis house (built in 1857). The front rooms of the Neoclassical mansion are restored and used for functions before and after performances. The auditorium is adroitly attached to the back of the house.

HERITAGE PLAZA (5)

100 Roosevelt Avenue
Telephone: (912) 432-6955
Museum open Mon-Sat 2:00-
5:00; planetarium open Sat
3:00; model train display, open
Wed, Sat, Sun 2:00-4:30
No charge for plaza; for plan-
etarium, Adults $1.50
Handicapped accessible
Age: Built in 1913 with later
additions
Style: Craftsman and others

Heritage Plaza

Heritage Plaza consists of a group of historic buildings gathered around the former train station. The centerpiece of the plaza is an impressive heavy-bracketed Craftsman style structure now used as the heritage museum and for social functions. Heritage Plaza contains an information center as well as several other buildings slated for rehabilitation.

ALBANY MUSEUM OF ART (6)

311 Meadowlark Drive
Telephone: (912) 435-0977 or
(912) 439-8400
Open Tues-Sun 12:00-5:00
Donation requested
Handicapped accessible
Architect: Mack Wakeford
Age: Built in 1983
Style: Modern

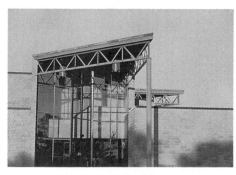

Albany Museum of Art

The Albany Museum of Art began humbly as the regional art association in an old hosiery warehouse in 1964. Since then it has become one of the state's visual arts powerhouses. Its present home is an angular modern building of utilitarian materials: exposed steel trusses, split-faced block, quarry tile, and concrete used with sufficient flair to avoid any Spartan feeling. The Albany Museum of Art is worth a visit several times a year for both its permanent collection and its aggressively sought visiting exhibits.

Nearby: MYRON BED & BREAKFAST (not on map) forty miles east of Albany, in Tifton, is a restored hotel. Convenient to I-75, it is located at 128 First Street, P.O. Box 264, Tifton, GA 31793. Telephone: (912) 382-0959.

KOLOMOKI MOUNDS STATE PARK (not on map), fifty miles west of Albany, has the largest group of Indian burial mounds in the state. They are located north of Blakely off US 27 in Early County. Address: Route 1, Blakely, GA 31723. Telephone: (912) 723-5296.

Americus (Sumter County)

Americus had its heyday in the 1890s and early 1900s as both farming and trade prospered in the area. Its architecture, in the blocks bounded roughly by Jackson, Forsyth, South, and Lamar Streets, reflects these past days of glory. Though several of the important buildings remain vacant, the recent rehabilitation of the WINDSOR HOTEL (1) could turn the tide toward a wider-scale downtown renaissance. The residential streets S. Lee, College, and Taylor and the neighborhood around Reese Park make for an excellent driving or walking tour. An April tour of historic homes is offered.

For information contact:
Americus-Sumter County Chamber of Commerce, P.O. Box 724, Americus, GA 31709; telephone (912) 924-2646; or Sumter Historic Preservation Society, P.O. Box 1416, Americus, GA 31709.

WINDSOR HOTEL (1)

Jackson Street at Windsor Avenue. Telephone: (912) 924-1555
Open all year
No admission fee. Handicapped accessible
Architect: G. L. Norrman; restoration by Anders Kaufmann, interiors by Design Solutions
Age: Built in 1892
Style: Combines several Victorian era styles

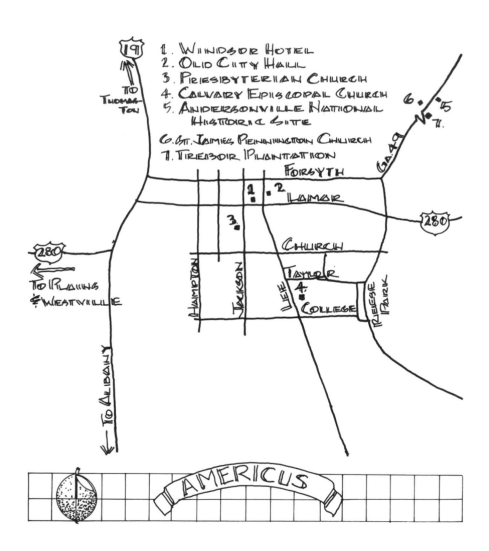

1. Windsor Hotel
2. Old City Hall
3. Presbyterian Church
4. Calvary Episcopal Church
5. Andersonville National Historic Site
6. St. James Pennington Church
7. Trebor Plantation

AMERICUS

With turrets, dormers, towers, arcades, bays, and balconies, the 80,000-square-foot Windsor is more like a small city than a hotel. Indeed, this wonderful conversation of forms takes up most of a city block. Built by overly optimistic entrepreneurs seeking to attract wintering Yankees, the Windsor failed to keep the Northerners from going on to Florida but succeeded as the center of Sumter County society. Its presence in downtown Americus is so dominating that it became the city's symbol even while it was closed for a number of years. A Herculean historic rehabilitation effort succeeded in reopening the hotel in late 1991.

Windsor Hotel

Nearby: OLD CITY HALL (2), 109 S. Lee Street (1891; G. L. Norrman, architect), is a solidly proportioned brick building with Roman temple elevations and Romanesque arched windows. The tapering or incline of the facades is a rare and effective device which emphasizes the building's masonry mass. Originally housing the police on the ground floor, city offices on the second, and a meeting room on the third, the building is now in private use as offices.

PRESBYTERIAN CHURCH (3), 125 S. Jackson Street (c. 1884), features fine wooden Carpenter Gothic details.

CALVARY EPISCOPAL CHURCH (4)

> 408 S. Lee Street. Telephone: (912) 924-3908
> Open Mon-Fri 9:00-12:00; and for services on Sun at 8:30 and 10:30
> No admission fee. Handicapped accessible
> Architect: Cram & Ferguson (Ralph Adams Cram), New York
> Age: Built in 1919
> Style: Gothic Revival

Deliberate understatement is such a rarity in church architecture that it is easily overlooked when encountered. The visitor to Calvary Episcopal should not make this mistake, however, for this little church was designed by one of the most celebrated and influential church architects in America. Ralph Adams Cram was not only the preeminent church designer of his day but was also the architect for Rice University and Princeton University and was one-time dean of Massachusetts Institute of Technology's school of architecture. A direct appeal from Calvary's rector, the Reverend Lawrence, led to Cram's accepting the commission for this small country chapel. The austerity of Calvary Church is a result of Cram's disdain for the excesses of the nineteenth century's Carpenter Gothic. Its exceeding simplicity of execution, however, is made profound by the authority of Cram's design and detailing.

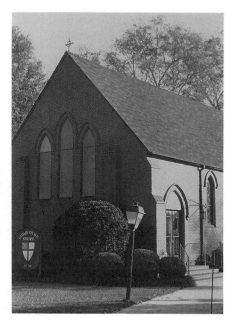

Calvary Episcopal Church

ANDERSONVILLE NATIONAL HISTORIC SITE (5)

Route 1, Box 85, Andersonville, GA 31711 (just over the line in Macon County)
Telephone: (912) 924-0343
Open every day 8:00-5:00
Donation requested. Handicapped accessible
Age: Begun in 1864

Though reminders of the Civil War permeate the state, nowhere is the full scale of its horror so palpable as it is in Andersonville. The site of Fort Sumter Civil War Prison, Andersonville today is a deceptively serene place: a rectangular, spring-fed 26-acre clearing in the rolling woodlands. The prison existed just fourteen months, yet the statistics it generated have impressed generations. In all, 45,000 prisoners were held at Andersonville; up to 26,000 were confined at one time; 13,000 never left.

The original prison walls, made of logs, are gone. A portion of the stockade has been recreated, and some of the fort's archaeology has been exposed to give the

Rostrum, Andersonville National Historic Site

visitor a sense of the place as it was. A number of fine memorials have been erected but none more impressive than the cemetery's Rostrum (1941). A raised Classical platform, the Rostrum is a place for reflection, looking out over the thousands of soldiers' graves, and is the center of Memorial Day services organized by the National Park Service.

Nearby: The town of Andersonville hosts a visitors center in a restored train depot. ST. JAMES PENNINGTON CHURCH (6) in Andersonville is Ralph Adams Cram's only log church, and he apparently designed it free of charge.

TREBOR PLANTATION (7), south of Andersonville on State 49 (1833 with many additions), is a working plantation open to visitors every day but Tuesday and holidays, 10:00-4:00. Adults $5.00. Telephone: (912) 924-6886.

WESTVILLE (not on map), S. Mulberry Street, Lumpkin, GA 31815 (35 miles west of Americus in Stewart County), is a living history village depicting a Georgia community in 1850. Telephone: (912) 838-6310; Open Mon-Sat 10:00-5:00, Sun 1:00-5:00; closed holidays. Adults $6.00, seniors $5.00, children $3.00.

PLAINS (not on map) is ex-President Jimmy Carter's hometown. Relive the good ol' days of 1976 in the town that looks just as it did when Billy Carter was pumping gas and Miss Lillian was enthralling visitors at the old train station. (US 280, 10 miles west of Americus.)

The Victorian Styles

"Victorian" is a catch-all word for a group of styles popular during the long reign of Queen Victoria. This period of architecture in America runs roughly from 1840 to 1910. The major Victorian styles found in Georgia are the Gothic Revival, Italianate, Second Empire, Octagon, Stick, and Queen Anne. Southwest Georgia, the area of the state least damaged by the Civil War, profitably developed its forest products, cotton, and tourism industries during the late Victorian period. The consequent prosperity created a demand for new buildings, and as a result, the towns in this region contain excellent examples of these styles.

The Gothic Revival was the first of the Victorian styles to develop. It was popularized in Britain as a way of expressing the genius of the Anglo-Saxon past. Characterized by pointed-arch windows and very steep roofs, it relied on little decoration to achieve its effect. The style can be seen primarily on unpretentious farm and town houses of the period. Saint John's Episcopal Church in Bainbridge is a more public example of the Gothic Revival.

The palaces of Italy served as the source for the vocabulary of the Italianate style. Buildings of this style feature round or segmented arched windows, square fronts, and bracketed eaves. The Italianate style found favor particularly in Columbus, where such well-preserved examples as the Springer Opera House and the Rankin House can be seen.

The Second Empire style's salient feature is a mansard roof. Popularized in Paris during the reign of Napoleon II, this style is rare in Georgia and is usually found mixed-in with Queen Anne elements.

A book by Orson S. Fowler, *The Octagon House: A Home For All,* created the philosophical underpinnings for the Octagon style. Fowler maintained that the octagon closely resembled nature's most perfect shape, the circle, and that many benefits flowed from this form. There are only a few hundred Octagon style buildings in the nation and fewer than a half dozen in Georgia. An Octagon building has been moved to the grounds of The Crescent in Valdosta, and Columbus has two Octagons: May's Folly (private) and Wynnwood.

Houses in which wood trim is employed to express the inner structure of the building are in the Stick Style. The expressed (not exposed) posts, beams, and braces would give the buildings a Tudor feeling were it not for the colorful paint schemes that go with the style. Thomasville's Lapham-Patterson House has many Stick style motifs.

The Queen Anne style is the most abundantly represented of the Victorian styles in Georgia. Entire neighborhoods in Bainbridge, Thomasville, and Valdosta are made up primarily of Queen Anne style homes. Incorporating elements from the other Victorian styles, the Queen Anne style typically features a deliberately asymmetrical massing, long wraparound porches, beadwork, and a turret or round shape somewhere in the composition. It came into popularity about 1880, when renewed prosperity following the Reconstruction period became widespread in the state.

West Georgia

Columbus (Muscogee County)

For information contact:
Georgia Visitors Center, 1751 Williams Road, Columbus, GA 31904, telephone
(706) 649-7455; Historic Columbus Foundation, telephone (706) 322-0756; or
Columbus Convention and Visitors Bureau, P.O. Box 2768, Columbus, GA
31902, telephone (706) 322-1613.

SPRINGER OPERA HOUSE (1)

103 Tenth Street. Telephone: (706) 324-5714
Open Wed and Sat for the 2-hour Heritage Tour which departs from the Georgia Visitors Center
at 10:00 A.M. It is also open for performances by the Springer Theater Company and Springer
Children's Theater
Heritage Tour admission: adults $5.00, students $2.50
Architect: Built by Francis J. Springer
Age: Built in 1871
Style: Italianate

The opera house is distinguished on its exterior by bracketed eaves and an elaborate iron balcony. Inside it is one of the finest nineteenth-century theaters in the South. The two balconies are outlined in tulip-shaped pin lights and supported by cast iron Corinthian columns and barrel-vaulted structure. Three-tiered box seats complete the unique auditorium space.

Springer Opera House

Nearby: **FIRST NATIONAL BANK BUILDING (2)**, Broadway at 11th, is the largest cast iron building left in the state. It was prefabricated in Pittsburgh on the eve of the Civil War.

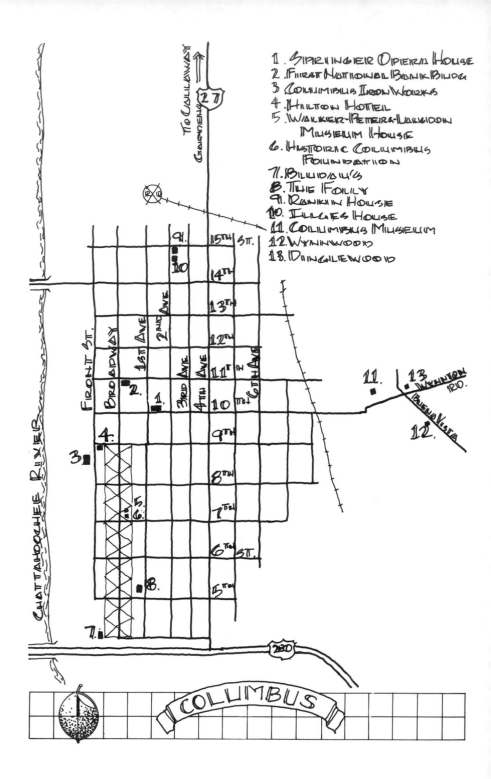

THE COLUMBUS IRON WORKS CONVENTION AND TRADE CENTER (3)

801 Front Avenue. Telephone: (706) 322-1613
Open Mon-Sat 9:00-5:00; also open for conventions
No admission fee. Handicapped accessible
Architect: Restoration by Pound, Flowers & Dedwyler
Age: Earliest structures date from 1853
Style: Nineteenth-century Industrial

The Iron Works is one of the state's most noteworthy rehabilitation projects. This former factory produced cannons and gunboats during the Civil War. Today the sensitive reworking of the building into a successful convention center has initiated the rediscovery of Columbus's riverfront.

Nearby: The Iron Works is at the north end of the Columbus Historic District, which runs down Broadway from Eighth Street to US 280. Along the way are the HILTON HOTEL(4), which is partially housed in an old factory building; the WALKER-PETERS-LANGDON MUSEUM (5), 716 Broadway, open Mon-Fri 10:00-4:00; the HISTORIC COLUMBUS FOUNDATION (6), 700 Broadway, open Mon-Fri 10:00-4:00; and BLUDAU'S RESTAURANT (7), 405 Broadway, open for lunch & dinner, telephone (706) 324-4863.

A rare example of the Octagon style can be seen in the 500 block of 1st Avenue. Known as THE FOLLY or MAY'S FOLLY (8), this private residence was built in 1861.

RANKIN HOUSE (9)

1440 Second Avenue. Telephone: (706) 322-0756
Open for the 2-hour Heritage Tour Wed & Sat and for special functions
Heritage Tour departs from the Georgia Welcome Center at 10:00 A.M.
Adults $5.00, students $2.50. Not handicapped accessible
Architect: Built by Lawrence Wimberly Wall for James Rankin;
restoration architect Edward Warner Neal
Age: Begun c.1860; construction not completed until after the Civil War
Style: Italianate

The Rankin house is maintained in excellent condition by the Junior League of Columbus. The first-floor front rooms have been restored to the house's original period.

Nearby: ILLGES HOUSE (10), 1428 Second Avenue, open Mon-Sat, 10:00-4:00, is a Corinthian-ordered Greek Revival house now open as an antique store. The original four-over-four section was built in 1850. The Italianate touches—cornice brackets and wrought iron—were added in subsequent renovations. Telephone: (706) 322-5324.

COLUMBUS MUSEUM (11), 1251 Wynnton Road, provides both art and history in its exciting new headquarters, which backs up to a garden designed by Frederick Law Olmstead's firm. The 1989 enlargement and restoration is by Hecht, Burgeshaw & Johnson architects with Cox Design consultants. The original building is by A. Ten Eyck Brown, architect. Telephone (706) 322-0400; open Tues-Sat 10:00-5:00, Sun 1:00-5:00; no admission fee; handicapped accessible.

WYNNWOOD (12)

1846 Buena Vista Road
Architect: Original
    section built by
    Lambert Spencer
Age: Center portion of
    building dates from
    1834; octagonal wings
    date from 1868
Style: Greek Revival,
    Italianate, and
    Octagonal

Wynnwood

Restored and kept in mint condition, Wynnwood is an example of the changes in architectural fashion that occurred in the nineteenth century. Grafted onto a petite Greek Revival house are matching octagonal end wings detailed in the Italianate style, which found so much currency in Columbus. Wynnwood housed a radio station but is now for sale.

Nearby: DINGLEWOOD (13), 1429 Dinglewood Street, is a private residence designed by Barrington & Morton of Columbus in 1859 for Joel Early Hurt. It is an Italianate masterpiece.

Meriwether, Harris, and Talbot Counties

For information contact:
Meriwether County Chamber of Commerce, P.O. Box 9, Warm Springs, GA 31830, telephone: (706) 655-2558.

MERIWETHER COUNTY COURTHOUSE (1)

Courthouse Square, Greenville
Open Mon-Fri 9:00-5:00
No admission fee
Architect: J. W. Golucke; restored
  in 1976 after a fire
Age: Built in 1903
Style: Neoclassical

J. W. Golucke designed a number of courthouses in the state. This building with giant Corinthian columns and a handsome dome structure with clock and bell tower is one of his best.

Meriwether County Courthouse

LITTLE WHITE HOUSE (2)

GA Highway 85W, south of Warm Springs, GA 31830. Telephone: (706) 655-3511
Open daily 9:00-5:00 except Thanksgiving and Christmas; last tour begins at 4:15
Adults $3.00, children $1.50. Handicapped accessible
Architect: Henry Toombs
Age: Built in 1932
Style: Neoclassical

Though it is a well constructed and proportioned cottage, the Little White House is distinguished chiefly by the fact that its builder and owner was Franklin Delano Roosevelt. The delight of the place comes from the awareness that the affairs of state could well be carried out in such unpretentious surroundings. The adjacent museum is worth a few minutes' time because it provides an understanding of the area's place in history.

For further information contact:
The Georgia Department of Natural Resources, toll free: in Georgia (800) 3GA-PARK, outside Georgia (800) 5GA-PARK

Nearby: The town of **WARM SPRINGS (3)** was made internationally famous in the 1930s by Roosevelt's patronage. Its thermal waters are still used for physical therapy and rehabilitation. The downtown is a mostly restored commercial block with buildings dating in origin from 1880 to 1910.

1. Meriwether County Courthouse
2. Little White House
3. Warm Springs
4. Sibley Horticultural Center
5. Butterfly House
6. General Store
7. Zion Episcopal Church
8. Talbot County Courthouse
9. Straus-Lievert Memorial Hall

GA 100
GA 109
LaGrange
GREENVILLE
ALT 27

GA 194
GA 85W
GA 18
LaGrange
PINE MTN.
5.
4.
CALLAWAY GARDENS
6.
GA 190
ROOSEVELT STATE PARK
2.
3.
WARM SPRINGS
MANCHESTER
ALT 27

27
COLUMBUS
TALBOTTON
8.
7.
9.
CLARK
80
80
THALINSON COLLEGE

MERIWETHER · HARRIS · TALBOT

Harris County

Callaway Gardens, a prime attraction in this county, is a 12,000-acre family-oriented resort with a number of fine pavilions and commercial buildings scattered throughout.

For information contact:
Callaway Gardens, Dept. X85, Pine Mountain, GA 31822.

JOHN A. SIBLEY HORTICULTURAL CENTER (4)

Callaway Gardens, Pine Mountain. Telephone: (706) 663-2281
Open seven days a week, Nov-Feb 8:00-5:00, Mar-Oct 7:00-6:00
Adults: $5.00; includes admission into Callaway Gardens Park
Handicapped accessible
Architects: Craig, Gaulden & Davis
Age: Built in 1984
Style: High-Tech

Callaway Gardens has created the ultimate greenhouse and Georgia's most eloquent High-Tech architectural statement at the Sibley Horticultural Center. The structure is of naturally rusting steel. Roof panels are double-walled translucent stretched fabric. The north walls are partly earth-bermed, partly glass block. Huge motor-operated glass and steel folding doors form the south wall. When the doors are open, the landscaped gardens and greenhouse become one.

Sibley Horticultural Center

Nearby: Also within the park, the **BUTTERFLY HOUSE (5)** (1990; Jova Daniels Busby, architects) is a building designed to display the life cycle of the butterfly. The **GENERAL STORE (6)**, on top of Pine Mountain, serves what may be the best breakfast in the state with a splendid view over Southwest Georgia.

Talbot County

ZION EPISCOPAL CHURCH (7)

Jackson Street, Talbotton
Open only occasionally for services
No admission fee. Not handicapped accessible
Age: Built c. 1850
Style: Gothic Revival

This unremodeled example of an early Gothic Revival parish church has an extant slaves' gallery and handmade walnut furnishings. As was not the case with other antebellum Gothic Revival buildings in the state, an attempt was made in Zion Episcopal Church to integrate and understand the nature of the style being employed. In other early works such as the Green-Meldrim house in Savannah and the Old State Capitol in Milledgeville, the creators essentially applied Gothic details to an otherwise Classically designed facade. Here the vertically applied, simple flush siding, pointed arch windows, and steep roof do justice with a minimum of means to the design potential of the style. Zion Episcopal Church

Zion Episcopal Church

reminds us that the philosophical basis for the Gothic Revival was in its ability to deliver elegance without pomposity or decoration. The Victorians' taste for the elaborate and exotic obscured the style's simple message.

Nearby: TALBOT COUNTY COURTHOUSE (8), Courthouse Square, Talbotton, is another Romanesque Revival courthouse by Bruce & Morgan (1892), Georgia's courthouse architects par excellence. Open Mon-Fri, 9:00-5:00.

The Greek Revival style STRAUS-LEVERT MEMORIAL HALL (9), College Street, has some unusual stylized Ionic capitols.

La Grange (Troup County)

For information contact:
La Grange area Chamber of Commerce, P.O. Box 636, 221 Bull Street, La Grange, GA 30241, telephone: (706) 884-8671

BELLEVUE (1)

205 Ben Hill Street.
Telephone: (706) 884-1832
Open Tues-Sat 10:00-12:00 and 2:00-5:00
Adults $1.50
Architect: Unknown
Age: Built in 1852; restored in 1975 by the Callaway Foundation
Style: Greek Revival

Bellevue

The former home of Georgia's "silver tongued orator," Senator Ben Hill , this is one of the few Greek Revival homes in the state that is not a remodeling of an older structure. The house is superbly sited at the end of a long, magnolia-lined alley. It is in the peristyle design and has hefty, fully developed Ionic columns, 36 inches in diameter. The ceilings on the first floor are 17 feet high. Magnificent door and window moldings carry pediments with dentils, cornice designs, and finials. The base molding is 2 feet tall. The house contains period furnishings and is administered by the La Grange Women's Club.

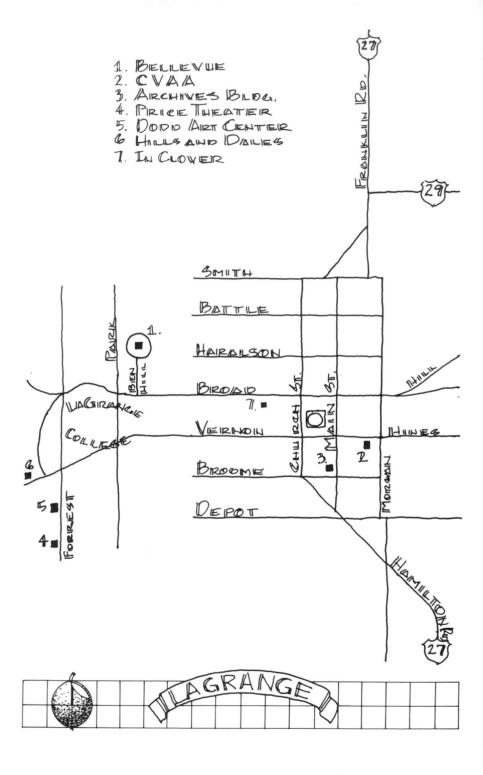

1. BELLEVUE
2. CVAA
3. ARCHIVES BLDG.
4. PRICE THEATER
5. DODD ART CENTER
6. HILLS AND DALES
7. IN CLOVER

CHATTAHOOCHEE VALLEY ART ASSOCIATION (CVAA) (2)

112 Hines Street. Telephone: (706) 882-2911
Open Tues-Sat 9:00-5:00, Sun 1:00-5:00
No admission fee. Handicapped accessible
Architect: Renovation architect Frank Traylor
Age: Built in 1892
Style: Gothic Revival

The CVAA proves you can make a silk purse out of a sow's ear. This sow's ear was a Victorian jail, now rehabilitated with such imagination and confidence as to overcome completely any negative associations with its past use. The makeover was not achieved without putting the building through some major changes. On the exterior, the brick walls and ashlar stone foundation were painted white, and a new standing-seam metal roof was installed. Some windows were bricked up; most have been reglazed in single panes of bronze-framed glass. In front a walled sculpture garden has been added. With the building's past use successfully deemphasized, a delightful play of textures and Victorian era forms emerges.

The interior was gutted to create the gallery spaces. Substantial use has been made of changing levels and surprise turns. This is not blank museum space but an interesting architectural space, a blending of old forms and rich modern materials.

TROUP COUNTY ARCHIVES BUILDING (3)

136 Main Street. Telephone: (706) 884-1828
Open Mon-Fri 9:00-5:00 except holidays
No admission fee
Architects: Hoggson Brothers, New York; renovation by Neal-Green & Clark
Age: Built in 1917; renovated in 1982
Style: Neoclassical

The Troup County Archives Building was originally commissioned by Fuller E. Callaway to house the La Grange Savings Bank and the Callaway corporate offices. The 1982 renovation converted the building into its present use.

PRICE THEATER (4)

La Grange College, 601 Broad Street, La Grange, GA 30240. Telephone: (706) 882-2911
Open for performances and during the school year for practices
Admission fee depends on performance. Handicapped accessible
Architect: Scarbrough & Associates
Age: Built in 1975
Style: Modern

The Price Theater illustrates many of the strengths of the Modernistic design approach. Its highly sculptural enclosure generates tremendous presence through inclined concrete walls and a monumental entrance. Though it is not a huge building, the attention-grabbing exterior creates architectural drama and expectation for the performances that take place inside.

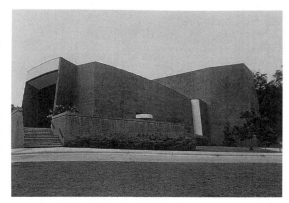

Price Theater

The interior does not continue the exterior's exuberance. Its appears neither excessively plain nor too ornate. It simply provides a comfortable, intimate space for the communication between performers and audience.

Nearby: Next door is the LAMAR DODD ART CENTER (5) (1982, also by Scarbrough & Associates), the college's museum. Open daily 10:00-4:00.

HILLS AND DALES (6), the Callaway mansion, 1200 Vernon Road, is architect Neel Reid's (Hentz, Reid, and Adler) masterpiece. The house is private, but the magnificent gardens are occasionally opened for viewing.

The IN CLOVER RESTAURANT (7), 205 Broad Street (1892), is a Queen Anne style former home. Open Mon-Sat for lunch and dinner. Telephone: (706) 882-0883.

Newnan (Coweta County)

Newnan and Coweta County benefit from Atlanta's prosperity without suffering many of the ills of suburbanization. Traffic is still manageable, the downtown is still used, and best of all, the neighborhoods of genteel homes are in great shape thanks to the continuing influx of people from the Atlanta market willing to invest their time and money in the "City of Homes." The visitor can leave in any direction from the Court Square to ride through interesting neighborhoods. Go north up Jefferson and College Streets, east out East Broad Street, Southwest out La Grange Street, and Southeast out Greenville Street.

For information contact:
Welcome Center, Newnan-Coweta Chamber of Commerce, P.O. Box 1103,
Newnan, GA 30264, telephone (706) 253-2270.

COWETA COUNTY COURTHOUSE (1)

Court Square, Newnan
Open Mon-Fri 9:00-5:00
No admission fee
Handicapped accessible
Architect: J. W. Golucke & Co.
Age: Built in 1904
Style: Neoclassical

The Coweta County Courthouse and town square form an attractive, vibrant center for Newnan. The 1989 restoration brought the courthouse up to code but left the exterior unchanged. A Neoclassical composition in red brick with limestone trim, the courthouse presents a civic face to each side of the square. The building's most distinctive design feature is the extensive use of copper. Its cornices, dentils, and clock tower are all sheathed in the metal.

Nearby: MALE ACADEMY MUSEUM (2), College Street at Temple Street, is a dignified, plain school building that contains exhibits highlighting the region's history. Newnan's role as a hospital town during the Civil War is particularly interesting. Telephone: (706) 251-0207; open Tues-Thurs 10:00-12:00, and 1:00-3:00, Sat & Sun 2:00-5:00; handicapped accessible.

PARROTT-CAMP-SOUCY HOUSE (3)

155 Greenville Street. Telephone:
(706) 253-4846
Call for an appointment to visit
Age: Built in 1855
Style: Eastlake and Second Empire

Coweta County Courthouse

73

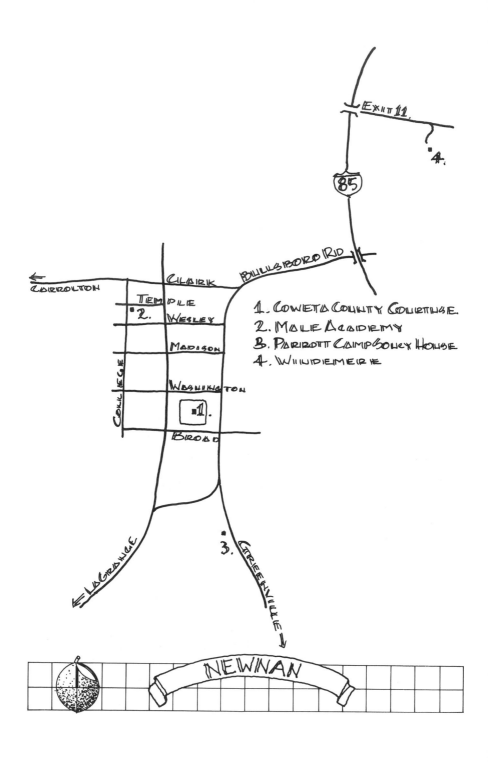

This magnificently restored home is now open as a bed and breakfast with two guest rooms. Its wonderfully restless design defies the eye to settle on one place in the facade. The compositon's complexity is allowed its fullest expression in the meticulous restoration work. The care put into the house's repainting deserves special mention.

WINDEMERE (4)

One mile east of I-85, Exit 11. Telephone: (706) 463-0940
Open by appointment only
Adults $5.00. Not handicapped accessible
Architect: William A. Yarbrough; restored in 1940 by John Eck
Age: Built in 1850
Style: Greek Revival

Parrot-Camp-Soucy House

This house was once the center of a 2,000-acre plantation. The Greek Revival building has a z-shaped, rather than the usual square, footprint. The first floor contains 11-foot ceilings, walnut trim, and heart-pine floors. Windemere is still a private residence, but visitors are welcome, if they call ahead, and special functions are held here as well.

Modern Architecture in Georgia

Fans of modern architecture wishing to see clean-lined, elegant, machine-precise contemporary design have virtually only one destination in Georgia: Atlanta. Do not pull into the average Georgia town or city expecting to find little-known treasures of modern vintage. Few architects outside Atlanta get much opportunity to work in the Modern style, and the Atlanta firms often seem to find little inspiration or encouragement outside the metro area.

Modernistic buildings that actually add to our smaller downtowns and our countryside are a rarity that this guide has endeavored to mention whenever possible. The few that do are often the work of smaller-town architects. West Georgia has fared better than other sections of the state in this regard. The Albany

Museum of Art, the Price Theater in La Grange, the Sibley Horticultural Center at Callaway Gardens in Harris County, and the Columbus Museum are four examples of architects' successful efforts to create something well above the ordinary.

The dearth of good Modern design in most of the state has begun to have its repercussions in the rapidly growing movement to institutionalize rejection of Modern styles of architecture. Style ordinances and review committees have begun to spring up primarily to keep out ugly, insensitively placed new buildings. This is a significant break with historic patterns of stylistic change in Georgia. More typically, developing styles were embraced precisely for their modernity and freshness.

One form of institutionalized rejection is the popular "Main Street" program adopted by many communities. Under this concept, attempts are made to rejuvenate downtowns by remolding them on a vision of a late-nineteenth-century town, from a master plan down to such details as reproduction street lamps. The idea is based on the premise that more people will use downtowns if a pleasing environment is created, and greater use will spur investment in the downtowns. The strength of the "Main Street" program lies in the fact that most of Georgia's towns and many of its buildings took shape during the period this concept seeks to imitate. Its obvious pitfall is that it offers little to stem the larger societal trends that have led people away from downtown and toward malls, strips, and office parks.

The premise of the Modern movement in architecture has helped to cause this situation. By throwing out many conventions of traditional architecture, it ushered in a period of tremendous experimentation and change. Any such movement is bound to create more duds than firecrackers. Outside Atlanta the opportunites for architects to experiment with Modernism and create distinctive works have been limited. Atlanta too has more ordinary and indifferent Modern buildings than treasures. The city has grown so rapidly during the last fifty years, however, that the treasures have begun to increase in number and impart to Atlanta a Modernistic sparkle that contrasts increasingly sharply with the heirloom gems offered by the rest of the state.

Central Georgia

Macon (Bibb County)

The new and old coexist happily in downtown Macon. Buildings date from the 1830s to the present and embrace a number of styles. Wide streets with parks, greenery, fountains, and monuments make the downtown a conducive setting for extensive rehabbing by private interests. These elements formed the backdrop for the most successful "Main Street" revitalization in the state. The "Main Street" formula employs such nineteenth-century elements as brick pavers, trees, street lamps, and benches to add detail and amenity to downtowns. Orchestrated properly, it can soften what is frequently a harsh downtown environment. Though Macon's downtown is not without its spotty sections, the blocks along Poplar, Cherry, and Mulberry Streets between M. L. King Boulevard and Spring Street have achieved an overall success that other Georgia towns would seek to emulate.

For information contact:
Macon-Bibb County Convention & Visitors Bureau, 200 Coliseum Drive, Macon, GA 31201, telephone: (912) 743-3401; or the Macon Heritage Foundation, P.O. Box 6092, Macon, GA 31208, telephone: (912) 742-5084.

WOODRUFF HOUSE (1)

988 Bond Street. Telephone: (912) 753-2715
Open for special tours; contact the Macon Heritage Foundation (see above)
Adults $1.00. Handicapped accessible
Architects: Elam Alexander; restoration by Brittain, Thompson, & May; interiors by Doris M. Schuler
Age: Built in 1836
Style: Greek Revival

The Woodruff House stands proudly gleaming on its hill overlooking downtown Macon. Its Acropolis-like setting was probably not lost on its builder, who created here Macon's best Greek Revival home. The exterior features a full peristyle Doric colonnade encircling walls of scored stucco over brick. The interior is a standard four-over-four arrangement with a glorious circular staircase at the back of the central hall. This staircase rises three stories and is crowned by a coffered cupola, through which ample daylight spills down the stair and into the

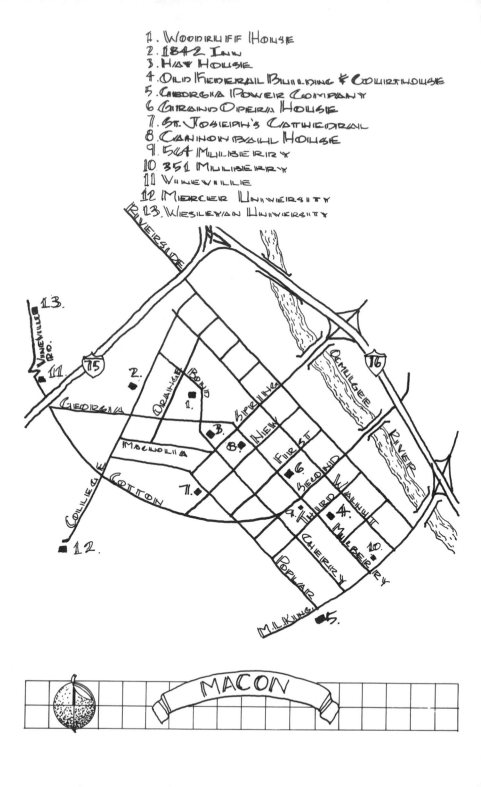

1. WOODRUFF HOUSE
2. 1842 INN
3. HAY HOUSE
4. OLD FEDERAL BUILDING & COURTHOUSE
5. GEORGIA POWER COMPANY
6. GRAND OPERA HOUSE
7. ST. JOSEPH'S CATHEDRAL
8. CANNONBALL HOUSE
9. 544 MULBERRY
10. 351 MULBERRY
11. VINEVILLE
12. MERCER UNIVERSITY
13. WESLEYAN UNIVERSITY

MACON

Woodruff House

niches that enliven its walls. The interior is completely refurbished, the most interesting room being the library. Here the handsome woodwork has been stripped back to its natural grain and sealed. A large dining porch has been added on the rear where a ballroom used to be.

The Woodruff House is owned by the Mercer University School of Law. It is used for several Mercer-related functions, to house and entertain special guests, and as the home for the John Adams Sibley Institute for Public Affairs and the National Center for Constitutional Studies.

Nearby: In this neighborhood are a number of restored Greek Revival and Victorian era houses. The **1842 INN (2)**, 353 College Street, is a rehabilitated Greek Revival mansion.

HAY HOUSE (WILLIAM B. JOHNSTON HOUSE) (3)

934 Georgia Avenue. Telephone: (912) 742-8155
Open Tues-Sat 10:30-4:30, Sun 2:00-4:00, closed holidays
Adults $4.00, students $2.00; free to members of the Georgia Trust for Historic Preservation
Not handicapped accessible
Architect: Thomas Thomas & Son, New York
Age: Built in 1855-1860
Style: Italianate

The Hay House is one of the top landmarks in the state and an artistic triumph. Its impressive statistics are worthy of mention. Twenty-four rooms occupy its 18,000 square feet. The grandest room is the 54- by 24-foot ballroom/gallery. A 20,000-gallon copper water tank in the attic supplied flush plumbing to the house, and speaking tubes between floors served as an intercom system in the days before city water and electricity. Italian artisans were brought over to execute the ornate plasterwork. The dazzling technical virtuosity displayed in the ceiling moldings and door casings is not repeated in Georgia. It has been estimated that to recreate the house today would cost $25 million.

The exterior, a refreshingly lighthearted brick rendition of the

Hay House

Italianate style, is topped with a handsome two-story cupola. It is now in excellent condition thanks to its conservation by the Georgia Trust. Impressive progress has been made on the interior restoration but it is a long-term endeavor. The project has been as painstakingly slow as an archaeological dig, which in some ways it is. Uncovering original details and paint colors and matching construction techniques require precision and care. The Georgia Trust is to be much credited for its dedication.

Nearby: The downtown area has several fine old Neoclassical buildings. At Mulberry and Third is the OLD FEDERAL BUILDING AND COURTHOUSE (4) (1908).

The GEORGIA POWER COMPANY (5) building, Poplar at M. L. King Boulevard, is the old Terminus Station rehabilitated in 1986 by Dunwood, Beeland and Henderson, architects. Telephone

Old Federal Building and Courthouse

(912) 784-5900; Open Mon-Fri 9:00-5:00; No admission fee.

There are other interesting buildings downtown in a potpourri of styles. The GRAND OPERA HOUSE (6), 651 Mulberry (1884; restored in 1970), is open for shows and for tours Mon-Fri by appointment. Telephone (912) 745-7925.

SAINT JOSEPH'S CATHEDRAL (7), Poplar at New Street (1903), displays an ornate brick exterior with a huge rose window in the front facade. Brother Cornelius Otten, designer of Sacred Heart Cathedral in Augusta, designed and built this church.

A Greek Revival home, the CANNONBALL HOUSE (8), 856 Mulberry (1853), gets its name from the noble distinction of being the only house in Macon hit by a Union cannonball during the Civil War. It is now operated as a local Civil War museum. Telephone: (912) 745-5982; open Tues-Fri 10:00-1:00 and 2:00-4:00, Sat and Sun 1:30-4:30; adults $3.00.

An Italianate mercantile building, 564 MULBERRY (9), dates from 1859.

At 351 MULBERRY (10), at the corner of M. L. King Boulevard, is Stephens Smith & Associates' imaginative reuse of a gas station.

Out of the downtown area are several places of architectural interest. VINEVILLE (11) contains many rehabilitated early twentieth-century homes.

The old campus of MERCER UNIVERSITY (12), on College Street, is executed in a unique Victorian Gothic style.

WESLEYAN UNIVERSITY (13) is a Georgian-styled campus. Facing its main axis is the bold Philip Shutze-designed Horgan House (late 1920s, private), based on the Italian Baroque. Wesleyan's library (1928) is also by Shutze.

Milledgeville (Baldwin County)

As Georgia's antebellum state capital, Milledgeville inspired and developed good architecture well before most other Georgia towns. Since Milledgeville lost its status to Atlanta after the Civil War, the downtown area has largely escaped development pressures and would still be recognizable to someone who had traveled its streets in the 1840s. What remains of the pre-Civil War period is a town laid out with four large squares, streets 100 feet wide, blocks of dignified two-story Federal and Greek Revival style homes, and two structures of national significance, the OLD STATE CAPITOL (1) and the OLD GOVERNOR'S MANSION (2).

For information contact:
Chamber of Commerce, P.O. Box 751, Milledgeville, GA 31061, telephone (912) 453-9311.

Central Georgia

GEORGIA MILITARY COLLEGE (OLD STATE CAPITOL) (1)

Jefferson Street.
Telephone: (912) 453-3481
Open during school term
No admission fee
Handicapped accessible
Architects: Jett Thomas with
    John Scott; 1830s additions
    by Smart & Lane; burned in
    1884 and was rebuilt; restora-
    tion work done in 1943
Age: Built in 1807
Style: Gothic Revival

Georgia Military College

The Old State Capitol, now the Georgia Military College, is one of the two oldest major public buildings in the nation of the Gothic Revival style. Constructed in 1807, it was altered in the 1830s and again in the 1860s by Federal occupying forces, who added the gates.

Gothic elements in the Old State Capitol are applied to, rather than incorporated in, the building's design. The massing, layout, and construction are basically those of a Neoclassical building. The Gothic pointed-arch windows, crenellated parapets, and tower are anything but Classical. As it was enlarged, the building gained its Gothic towers and porches. This was an extremely early time frame for Gothic detailing to turn up on an American public building. What prompted Georgia's leaders to have their capitol executed in this style is unknown. What is certain is that this building presaged the flowering of the Gothic Revival in America by a full forty years.

Nearby: A group of private residences on South Liberty Street dates from the 1820s and from 1870 to 1890. Their characteristic white-painted clapboards and black shutters make for a delightful walking tour.

OLD GOVERNOR'S MANSION (2)

N. Clarke Street.
Telephone: (912) 453-4545

Old Governor's Mansion

1. GEORGIA MILITARY COLLEGE
2. OLD GOVERNOR'S MANSION
3. JOHN MARLOR HOUSE
4. STETSON-SANFORD HOUSE
5. MASONIC LODGE
6. ATKINSON HALL

MILLEDGEVILLE

Central Georgia

Open Tues-Sat 9:00-5:00, Sun 2:00-5:00
Admission $1.00. Not handicapped accessible
Architect: Charles B. Cluskey
Age: Built in 1838
Style: Greek Revival

The state fathers chose the most important architect then practicing in Georgia for the design of the Governor's Mansion. Charles B. Cluskey had been working in Savannah when he received this commission. What he created here is an exquisite series of spaces and a stylistically influential facade.

The front displays the first Greek Revival portico in the state, fully realized and beautifully executed. The glorious centerpiece of the building is the rotunda. Elements of this fine Jefferson-inspired design influenced Georgia's master builders for decades to come. The Old Governor's Mansion is now home to the presidents of Georgia College.

JOHN MARLOR HOUSE (3)

201 N. Wayne Street. Telephone: (912) 452-3950
Open Mon-Fri 9:00-5:00, Sat by appointment, Sun 3:00-5:30
Donation requested. Handicapped accessible
Architect: John Marlor
Age: Built in 1830
Style: Federal

The John Marlor House was originally a two-over-two dogtrot house (two rooms separated by a breezeway) which was enclosed and given a Federal portico by local architect Marlor.

Nearby: STETSON-SANFORD HOUSE (4), 601 N. Hancock Street (c. 1825), is also by John Marlor. Elliptical motifs are used inside and outside, in the porch ceiling, over the doors, in the hall arch, and on the staircase. Other interesting elements in this house are the reverse-fluted rectangular columns of Doric inspiration and the off-center entry hall. Opened by request. Telephone (912) 452-4637.

Another building by Marlor, The MASONIC LODGE (5), Hancock at Wayne (1834), is the oldest lodge in the state and features a three-story cantilevered staircase.

ATKINSON HALL, GEORGIA COLLEGE (6)

231 W. Hancock Street. Telephone: (912) 453-5350
Open Mon-Fri 9-5 during school term
No admission fee. Handicapped accessible

Georgia College

Architect: Bruce & Morgan, Atlanta
Age: Built in 1896
Style: Neoclassical

Atkinson Hall is the oldest building at the school. It forms the centerpiece of a handsome two-block-long row of Neoclassical terraces that accommodate dormitory rooms, classrooms, and offices.

Eatonton (Putnam County)

Eatonton is an important stop on the antebellum trail and is the birthplace of Joel Chandler Harris. Though the town has not caught up with its neighbors Milledgeville and Madison for the quantity of its architectural offerings, it does feature a highly regarded home tour each year.

For information contact:
Eatonton Chamber of Commerce, P.O. Box 4088, Eatonton, GA 31024; telephone (706) 485-7701.

NAPIER-REID-RAINEY-BRONSON-STUBBS HOUSE (1)

114 Madison Avenue
Telephone: (706) 374-6383
Open Tues-Sat 1:00-5:00
No admission fee
Not handicapped accessible
Architect: Andrew Reid
Age: Original Piedmont Plain style house was built in the 1820s; remodeled in 1852 by Reid
Style: Greek Revival

This house is a stylistic hybrid showing influences from all the antebellum styles.

Napier-Reid-Rainey-Bronson-Stubbs House

85

Central Georgia

Its restoration by the Eatonton-Putnam Historical Society is ongoing.

Nearby: PUTNAM COUNTY COURTHOUSE (2) (1905; J. W. Golucke, architect) is at the corner of Jefferson and Sumter. Open Mon-Fri 9:00-5:00.

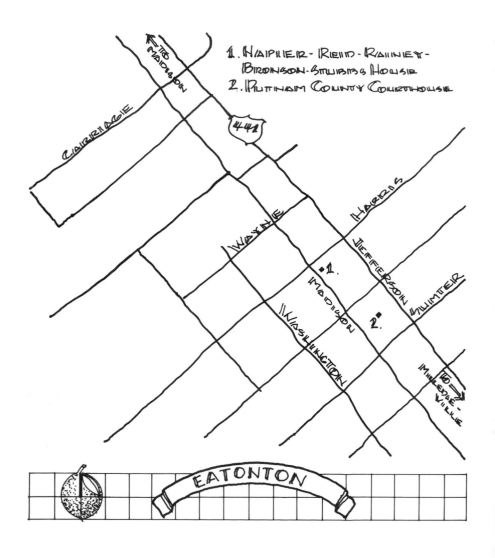

The Persistence of the Greek Revival

The towns of central Georgia, from Macon to Athens, are said to be on the "Antebellum Trail." These communities prospered as mercantile and administrative centers during the ascendency of the cotton economy, and they were spared the brunt of Sherman's campaigns. As a result, this region has the state's best collection of homes from the heyday of the Old South. The buildings from this period are characteristically in the style called Greek Revival.

Though it by no means originated in Georgia, the Greek Revival style found its full flowering here and in other Southeastern cotton states during the three decades preceding the Civil War. So successful was the style in dominating the architecture of the period that it has become the definitive image of the antebellum South. Imagery, however, is only part of the story.

During the early 1800s America was a nation searching for an architecture expressive of its political ideals. The architecture of the first democracy, ancient Athens, was well suited for this need. Simple and impressive, it made a connection between the Modern and Classicical periods. The style was first introduced in Georgia in the 1830s, about ten years after its introduction in the North.

The Greek Revival's essential element is a front porch colonnade at least the full width of the house (and preferably down the sides) holding up a heavy entablature. The columns are in one of the classical orders or, for those of limited means, some simplification of Classicism. The colonnade has been executed at all levels of sophistication in the South, from the amateurish to examples so lavish and accomplished as to rival those in Greece.

The Greek Revival style rooted sucessfully in Georgia because it filled several needs. It worked well incorporated into additions and remodeling efforts (which then as now accounted for much of the building activity). Neither a professional nor an artist was needed to add a Greek portico, and even a clumsily built example had a good effect from a distance. Further, the style's deep porches helped to temper the hot climate: colonnades provided welcome outdoor shade as well as shading for the interior spaces. Finally, imagery played an important role. Neighbors and visitors could easily appreciate the impressive, gleaming white Greek Revival houses against the landscape. These buildings spoke of dominance and mastery; they also spoke of culture and elegance.

The Civil War spelled the style's demise. As the postwar economy began its shift from rural agrarian to urban, the Greek Revival suddenly became the symbol of a day and ruling class gone by. The new leaders would be looking for something that would allow for more variety and individuality, something expressive of the new economic and social orders. This was the social climate into which the Victorian styles entered.

The Greek Revival continues to exert its powerful presence in the state with mixed effect. On the one hand, it is the symbol of a time when one race enslaved another. On the other, the sight of one of these grand homes under a canopy of pecan trees is one of Georgia's most memorable images.

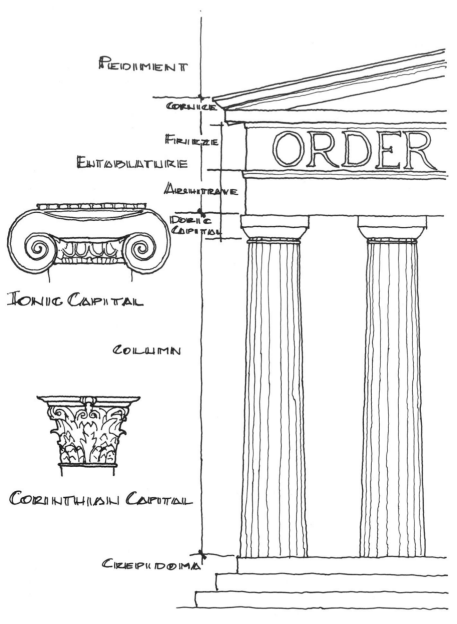

PEDIMENT

CORNICE

FRIEZE

ENTABLATURE

ARCHITRAVE

DORIC
CAPITAL

ORDER

IONIC CAPITAL

COLUMN

CORINTHIAN CAPITAL

CREPIDOMA

CLASSICAL ELEMENTS

Madison (Morgan County)

Several legends exist concerning why Madison was spared by Sherman on his infamous march to the sea. One postulates a love affair between the general and a lady from Madison who interceded on the town's behalf. Perhaps it was then, as it is now, simply too lovely a place to disturb.

The stately nineteenth-century homes which give Madison its unique flavor were generally the town homes for wealthy plantation owners. Many other fine homes were built by professionals and merchants enjoying the prosperity of the region. Madison's two great building periods, the 1830s–1860s and the 1880s–1910s, can be attributed to the cotton industry. The vagaries of the boll weevil and the advent of the Great Depression caused Morgan County, like many of the state's other agrarian-based counties, to lose half of its population in this century. It did not begin to recover until the 1960s.

A high degree of civic pride has helped this community retain its beautiful old homes. A walk or drive through Madison today is a stroll through a living museum of two of Georgia's finest periods in architecture: the Greek Revival and the Victorian. The homes in the downtown area should be seen on a walking tour. The speed of a car is too great to allow the visitor to savor the scale and wealth of detail this district offers.

For information contact:
Madison-Morgan Cultural Center, 434 South Main Street, Madison, GA 30650, telephone: (706) 342-4743. The Center is open weekdays from 10:00 to 4:30 and Sat-Sun from 2:00 to 4:00.

MADISON NATIONAL HISTORIC DISTRICT (1-26)

Madison opens itself up for visitors like no other town in Georgia. Private residences can be seen during the spring tour of homes in May, the theater festival tour in August, and the Christmas tour in December. A tour can be counted on to provide plenty of highlights and to operate like a well-oiled machine.

For more information contact:
The Morgan County Historical Society, 227 S. Main Street, Madison, GA 30650, can arrange for tour groups at other times. Admission fee for the tour of homes is approximately $6.00 Age: Buildings represent the entire nineteenth century.

BILLUPS HOUSE (1), 651 N. Main Street (1850), in contrast to the Jeptha-Vining-Harris House (2), illustrates the scale problems of a fully developed entablature on a one-story residence. The front gable helps to relieve the resulting horizontality.

JEPTHA-VINING-HARRIS HOUSE (2), 611 N. Main Street, was constructed in

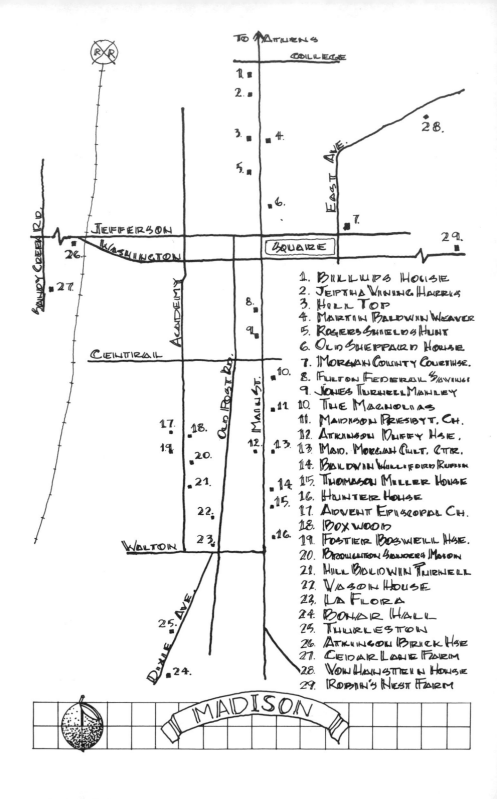

TO ↑ ATHENS

COLLEGE

1.
2.

3.   4.

5.

6.

EAST AVE.

7.

28.

29.

JEFFERSON
WASHINGTON   SQUARE
26.
27.

ACADEMY

CENTRAL

8.
9.

10.

11.

17.   18.
19.   20.
21.
22.
23.

OLD POST RD.

MAIN ST.

12.   13.

14.
15.

16.

WALTON

SANDY CREEK RD.

25. AVE.
DIXIE AVE.

24.

1. BILLUPS HOUSE
2. JEPTHA VINING HARRIS
3. HILL TOP
4. MARTIN BALDWIN WEAVER
5. ROGERS SHIELDS HUNT
6. OLD SHEPPARD HOUSE
7. MORGAN COUNTY COURTHSE.
8. FULTON FEDERAL SAVINGS
9. JONES TURNELL MANLEY
10. THE MAGNOLIAS
11. MADISON PRESBYT. CH.
12. ATKINSON DUFFY HSE.
13. MAD. MORGAN CULT. CTR.
14. BALDWIN WILLIFORD RUFFIN
15. THOMASON MILLER HOUSE
16. HUNTER HOUSE
17. ADVENT EPISCOPAL CH.
18. BOXWOOD
19. FOSTER BOSWELL HSE.
20. BROUGHTON SANDERS MASON
21. HILL BALDWIN TURNELL
22. VASON HOUSE
23. LA FLORA
24. BONAR HALL
25. THURLESTON
26. ATKINSON BRICK HSE
27. CEDAR LANE FARM
28. VON HANSTEIN HOUSE
29. ROBIN'S NEST FARM

MADISON

1850. The creator of this Greek Revival one-story cottage solved the often-addressed scale problem of a Classical portico and entablature in a one-story residence. Though small by Madison standards, the house holds its own for refinement of detail and elegance of scale.

Jeptha-Vining-Harris House

HILL TOP (3), 543 N. Main Street (1833), retains its Plantation Plain style character with a sensitive addition of a one-story Greek-columned front porch.

MARTIN-BALDWIN-WEAVER HOUSE (4), 488 N. Main Street (1850), has been justly hailed as one of the most fully realized examples of Greek Revival architecture in the state. Well-proportioned Doric columns across the front and a fully scaled entablature are the important elements of this house's quality.

THE ROGERS-SHIELDS-HUNT HOUSE (5), 503 N. Main Street, dates from 1815 but has later additions. The original home was a two-story log cabin with an open dogtrot. Additions framed around the dogtrot house create the current Plantation Plain style home. The low brick wall was a 1960s addition.

The unusual and overscaled mansard roof of the OLD SHEPPARD HOUSE (6), 340 N. Main Street, was added c. 1904.

The MORGAN COUNTY COURTHOUSE (7), E. Jefferson Street on the Square (1905; J. S. Golucke & Company, architects), displays an angled main facade in response to its out-of-the-way location on a back corner of the square and features a handsome arcaded entry, tower, and dome. Open Mon-Fri 9:00-5:00.

FULTON FEDERAL SAVINGS AND LOAN (8) (MARTIN L. RICHTER HOUSE), 201 S. Main, dates from the 1850s and was extensively remodeled in 1885. Open Mon-Fri 9:00-4:00.

JONES-TURNELL-MANLEY HOUSE (9), also called HERITAGE HALL, 227 S. Main (c.1835), is in the Greek Revival style and is now home to the Morgan County Historical Society.

THE MAGNOLIAS (10), S. Main Street, now the Saint James Catholic Mission, was built in 1860 and remodeled in 1880 in the Queen Anne style.

MADISON PRESBYTERIAN CHURCH (11), 383 S. Main Street, was built in1842. The simple interior, with its still existing slave gallery, is highlighted by Tiffany stained-glass windows. Open for services.

ATKINSON-DUFFY HOUSE (12), 433 S. Main Street, was built in 1850. Several additions have made this house a somewhat eclectic combination of Classical and Victorian elements. The Ionic-colonnaded one-story porch competes with the widow's walk for attention in this unique house.

MADISON-MORGAN CULTURAL CENTER (13), 434 S. Main, is a rehabilitated old school building. It houses an art gallery, a museum of history, a theater, and a reception room. Open weekdays 10:00-4:00, Sat-Sun 2:00-4:00.

BALDWIN-WILLIFORD-RUFFIN HOUSE (14),472 S. Main Street (1840s), is the only building left from the Georgia Female College.

The restrained exterior of the THOMASON-MILLER HOUSE (15), 498 S. Main Street, belies the wealth of Victorian era details on the interior.

HUNTER HOUSE (16), 280 S. Main Street (1883), is one of the best examples from the Victorian period in the state.

ADVENT EPISCOPAL CHURCH (17), 338 Academy Street, dates from 1840. The interiors are by Thomas Little. Open for services.

BOXWOOD (18), 375 Academy Street (1851), is named for its grounds, which were reputed to contain the finest boxwood gardens in Georgia. This unique Italianate house has been featured in many publications. The third floor is a ballroom with bandstand. Boxwood is not generally open.

Many additions and remodelings have made the FOSTER-BOSWELL HOUSE (19), 292 Academy Street, among the largest of the downtown residences.

Broughton-Sanders-Mason House

BROUGHTON-SANDERS-MASON HOUSE (20), 411 Old Post Road (1850), with its flanking gazebos, has on its porches some of the most delicate and elegant Victorian era carving to be found anywhere.

JOSHUA HILL-BALDWIN-TURNELL HOUSE (21), 485 Old Post Road (c. 1850), is a grand example of the Greek Revival and is frequently on the home tour.

VASON HOUSE (22), 549 Old Post Road, one of Madison's oldest, is basically a Piedmont Plain style house with a Classical porch added. The formal gardens, easily seen from Old Post Road, are beautiful.

LA FLORA (23), 601 Old Post Road (1895), is one of the youngest houses in the district. It has a well-proportioned and relatively restrained Victorian interior.

Joshua Hill-Baldwin-Turnell House

BONAR HALL (24), Dixie Avenue (1832), is a brick Georgian style home made particularly impressive by the successful addition of the Victorian porches in 1880. The contrast of the restrained brickwork with the lacy painted porches gives this composition real life.

THURLESTON (25), 847 Dixie Avenue, dates from 1800 with a major addition in 1848. The house's facade is enhanced by the use of pilasters instead of a large front porch, and an unusual three-gable roofline. Its placement at the end of a long shrub-lined allée gives this house extraordinary presence.

ATKINSON BRICK HOUSE (26), W. Washington Street, is so named because a brick home from the early 1800s is so rare. The Gothic gables and front porch were later additions.

HOMES OUTSIDE THE MADISON NATIONAL HISTORIC DISTRICT

CEDAR LANE FARM (27), 3790 Sandy Creek Road. The meticulous restoration of this Plantation Plain style farmhouse has been heralded in many publications. Interiors are of unpainted heart pine. The kitchen wing and modern conveniences have been sensitively added. The house is part of a working farm.

VON HANSTEIN HOUSE (28), 766 East Avenue, was built in1805 with Greek Revival additions. It is exquisitely sited at the end of a long perspective framed by mature hardwoods.

ROBIN'S NEST FARM (29), 2550 Bethany Road, dates from 1832 with Greek Revival additions. Flanked by long rows of cedars, this is a fully developed Greek Revival plantation house. Finely sculpted Ionic columns on the front support a well-proportioned and detailed entablature which engages all sides of the house.

Covington (Newton County)

Covington is one of those genteel, small Georgia towns that, like Roswell before it, seems destined to become swallowed up in Atlanta's suburban sprawl. Before it succumbs, the visitor can enjoy a leisurely tour and imagine without too much strain what the town was like a century ago. Switch on an episode of "In the Heat of the Night," which was filmed in Covington, for an armchair tour.

The best collections of nineteenth-century homes are on Floyd Street heading east of the town square and on Monticello Street heading south. A unifying element among Covington houses is the use of fanlights above doorways and first-floor windows.

Although no regular home tours are offered locally, several Atlanta convention tour companies arrange visits in some of the private residences. Many date from the 1840s and 1850s, and are in the Greek Revival and later styles.

Among those often visited are WHITEHALL (1), 2176 Monticello Street, and DIXIE MANOR (2), 3115 Pennington Street (c. 1850), a grand two-story Greek Revival home in brick.

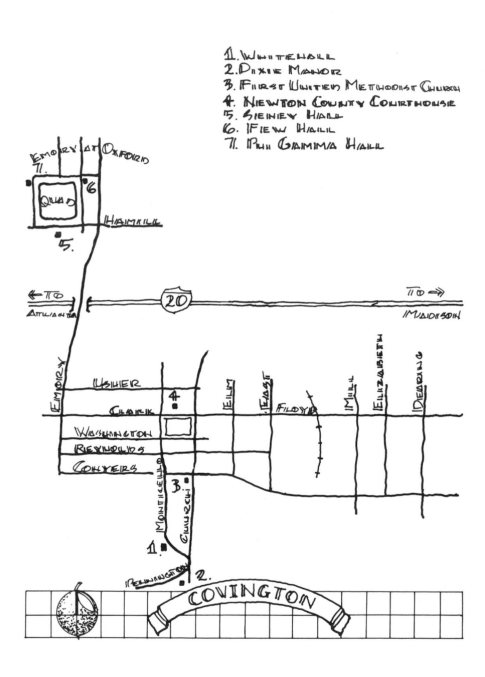

1. WHITEHALL
2. DIXIE MANOR
3. FIRST UNITED METHODIST CHURCH
4. NEWTON COUNTY COURTHOUSE
5. STONEY HALL
6. FEW HALL
7. PHI GAMMA HALL

EMORY AT OXFORD
7.

QUAD
6.

HAMILL
5.

← TO
ATLANTA
20
TO →
MADISON

EMORY

USHER

CLARK
4.

ELM

EAST

FLOYD

HULL

ELIZABETH

DEARING

WASHINGTON

REYNOLDS

CONYERS

MONTICELLO

3.

CHURCH

1.

PENNINGTON
2.

COVINGTON

FIRST UNITED METHODIST CHURCH (3)

1117 Conyers Street
Telephone: (706) 232-5342
Open Mon-Fri 9:00-5:00, and for
  Sunday services
No admission fee
Handicapped accessible
Architect: Unknown
Age: Built in 1854 to 1856 with later
  additions

This is one of the most pure expressions of the Greek Revival in an ecclesiastical building.

NEWTON COUNTY COURTHOUSE (4)

Clark Street, on the square
Open Mon-Fri 9:00-5:00
No admission fee
Architects: Bruce & Morgan
Age: Built in 1884
Style: Mixed Victorian Styles

First United Methodist Church

This is another turn-of-the-century brick courthouse building by the prolific firm of Bruce and Morgan. The well-preserved exterior is crowned by a handsome tower.

EMORY AT OXFORD (5-7)

Emory University, Oxford College, Seney Hall, Oxford, GA 30267
Telephone: (706) 786-7051

Across Interstate 20 from Covington, in Oxford, is the small campus of Emory at Oxford, Emory University's original location. On the college quadrangle is SENEY HALL (5) (1881), the administration building. The exterior has been beautifully rehabilitated to show off the proud, elongated proportions of this Victorian Gothic brick and stone building. The interior has been completely remodeled.

Other noteworthy campus buildings include FEW HALL (6) (1852) and PHI GAMMA HALL (7) (1851), which face each other across the quadrangle. Both are outstanding and rare examples of the Greek Revival employed for something other than residences and churches. Phi Gamma Hall was built to house a debating society. Few Hall was built to house the Few Society, an outgrowth of Phi Gamma.

Athens (Clarke County)

The Downtown Athens Historic District is a vibrant, compact urban area bounded by Broad, Lumpkin, Hancock, and Thomas Streets. The University of Georgia, across the street from downtown Athens, has helped downtown Athens maintain the active street life and pedestrian-oriented environment that make this area so successful. Athens was established in 1801, but most buildings date from 1890-1915. A few are pre-Civil War. The best times to catch everything open are during business hours, Monday through Friday.

For information contact:
Athens Convention & Visitors Bureau, P.O. Box 948, Athens, GA 30603, telephone (706)546-1805.

ATHENS WELCOME CENTER (CHURCH-WADDEL-BRUMBY HOUSE) (1)

280 E. Dougherty Street,
Athens, GA 30601
Telephone: (706) 353-
    1820
Open Mon-Sat 9:00-
    5:00, Sun 2:00-5:00
No admission fee
Age: Built in 1820
Style: Federal

Athens Welcome Center

Visitors to Athens should make this a first stop for tourist information and a concise guided tour of the house. The oldest residential structure in the city, this building has been beautifully restored and furnished by the Athens-Clarke Heritage Foundation. As the home of early University of Georgia presidents, the house occupies an important place in local history.

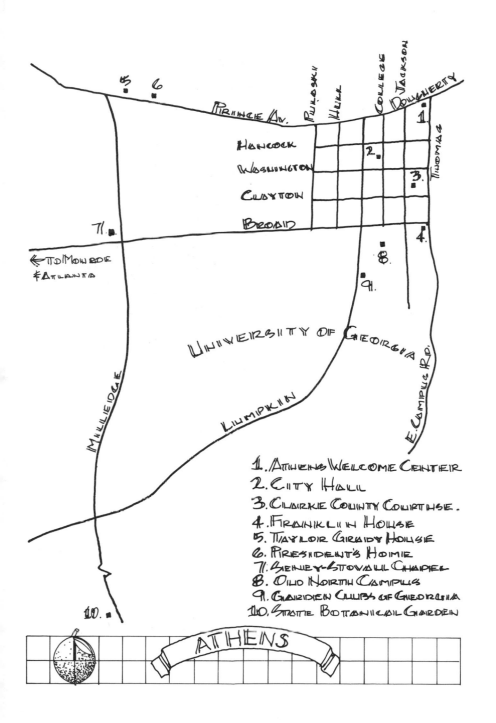

1. Athens Welcome Center
2. City Hall
3. Clarke County Courthse.
4. Franklin House
5. Taylor Grady House
6. President's Home
7. Sewey-Stovall Chapel
8. Old North Campus
9. Garden Clubs of Georgia
10. State Botanical Garden

ATHENS

CITY HALL (2)

College Avenue at Washington Street
Open Mon-Fri 9:00-5:00
No admission fee.
Handicapped accessible
Architect: L. F. Goodrich, Augusta
Age: Built in 1904
Style: Neoclassical

City Hall

The City Hall site is unjustly more famous for the bizarre double cannon out front than it is for the good, old-fashioned civic-mindedness displayed in its design. This long two-story building has entrances on all four sides. The horizontality of its plan is relieved by the handsome domed clock tower at its center.

Fanlit doorways lead to an interior that has dignity without any hint of pomposity. Tiled floors and plain moldings carry out the theme of simplicity down the long, straight corridors serving the various departments. The directness with which this structure houses city government and makes it available to people points up just how labyrinthine, difficult, and ultimately undemocratic so many of our government buildings have become.

CLARKE COUNTY COURTHOUSE (3)

Washington Street at Jackson Street
Open Mon-Fri 9:00-5:00
No admission fee. Handicapped accessible
Architects: A. Ten Eyck Brown; additions by Jenkins & Tyree, Charlotte
Age: Built c. 1914
Style: Neoclassical

Modern additions to our favorite civic buildings so often detract from the originals that when an addition actually adds to a building's character, the results are surprising. The Clarke County Courthouse was one of Brown's more mundane efforts until it was incorporated in a new conversation of forms and spaces introduced by the addition. The new building adroitly met a triple challenge by fitting in well with the original, organizing the vastly expanded space, and being interesting in its own right. The addition designers generally maintained the form and height of the older structure but added new materials and amplified details to create an expression distinct from the older building. Outside, the relationship between the new structure and the old is simultaneously appreciative and teasing, like that in a healthy parent-child relationship. Inside, however, the original and the addition regard each other across an atrium space in a less successful composition. There is little dialogue here. The atrium is too sparely designed to become an interesting element in its own right and so acts only as a gulf between old and new.

Nearby: The most interesting commercial building on Broad Street was for a long time under threat of demolition. The FRANKLIN HOUSE (4) at 480 Broad Street (c. 1845) was an early mixed-use complex designed to house shops on the first floor and a hotel on the second. Though there is no outside entrance to the second floor, its former importance is evidenced by the grandness and openness of the second-floor facade. The building was saved and renovated for offices in the 1980s.

TAYLOR-GRADY HOUSE (5)

> 634 Prince Avenue. Telephone: (706) 549-8688
> Open Mon-Fri 10:00-3:30. The house is frequently booked for private functions, so it is advisable to call ahead before visiting.
> Adults $2.50. Not handicapped accessible
> Age: Built in mid 1840s
> Style: Greek Revival

The Taylor-Grady house was built as the Greek Revival summer home of Robert Taylor. Later it became the family's principal residence. From 1865 until 1868 it was the home of Henry Grady, the influential managing editor of the *Atlanta Constitution* and the state's most famous orator. The house went through a devastating period of neglect during the 1950s and '60s during which it was thoroughly vandalized and stripped of all its furnishings. The porch and colonnade probably would have fallen in had the thirteen columns surrounding the home not been made of brick instead of wood. The Junior League and City of Athens joined together in 1968 to begin the building's rescue.

Today the Taylor-Grady House is one of the state's most accomplished restoration projects. It has become an important place for public functions. Weddings, meetings, and receptions of all kinds are hosted in the refurbished interiors and on the well-kept grounds.

Central Georgia

Nearby: The UNIVERSITY OF GEORGIA PRESIDENT'S HOME (6), 570 Prince Avenue (1858), is a wonderfully maintained Corinthian style Greek Revival home. It is occasionally opened for tours and public functions.

SENEY-STOVALL CHAPEL (7)

Milledge at Broad Street. The chapel was undergoing the final stages of restoration in 1992.
Architect: W. W. Thomas
Age: Begun in 1882

This unusual Victorian era chapel is in plan two nested octagons. The larger encloses the nave, or seating area, while the smaller one forms the pulpit. The chapel is part of a larger complex of the former Lucy Cobb Institute for girls, which is undergoing development and rehabilitation by the University of Georgia.

OLD NORTH CAMPUS HISTORIC DISTRICT (8)

Area bounded by Broad, Lumpkin, and Franklin Streets
Open every day
No admission fee. Handicapped accessible

Old North Campus Historic District

Age: The campus layout dates from 1785. The famous arch dates from 1857; the Chapel and
Demosthenian Hall are from the same period
Style: Mostly Greek Revival and Neoclassical

The University of Georgia campus began as a neatly organized group of buildings enclosing a verdant quadrangle. The chapel exemplifies the dignity and grace with which the buildings and landscape coexist. This simple, serene Greek Revival building performs two architectural roles. It is attractive in its own right as an object on the green and also functions as part of the background in the quadrangle enclosure. Its portico and short flight of stairs are mediating elements that belong equally to the building and the campus. The chapel is open during the day and used for many programs. One is as likely to hear the strains of flute practice floating out its doors as to hear a religious program.

As educational offerings and demands mushroomed in the twentieth century, this idyllic setting for learning gave way to an incomprehensible scattering of buildings. Like that of so many other universities, the University of Georgia's growth has completely overwhelmed the pattern and confines of the original campus plan. Perhaps it is no one's fault that the original campus plan could not be extended to accommodate such growth, but one must wonder how so many imposing structures could have been built with so little attention paid to their architectural potential. These buildings go up willy-nilly; the campus suffers, the students and faculty make do, and we all get less than we could have. Certainly no one has the excuse that the project was not begun well. The part of the campus extending from Broad Street to the library is handsome and worth visiting. The remainder is to be seen strictly as utility requires.

Nearby: GARDEN CLUBS OF GEORGIA (9) is headquartered in a restored house at 325 South Lumpkin Street. Telephone: (706) 542-3631. Open Mon-Fri 9:00-12:00 and 1:00-4:00; closed holidays. Architectural design consultant: Ed Wade.

Go south on Milledge Avenue to see the STATE BOTANICAL GARDEN (10). The Visitors Center/Conservatory, 2450 South Milledge Avenue (1985; Hall, Norris, & Marsh, architects), presents a tropical garden in a High-Tech enclosure. Telephone: (706) 542-1244; open Mon-Sat 9:00-4:30, Sun 11:30-4:30; handicapped accessible.

McDANIEL-TICHENOUR HOUSE (not on map), 30 miles west of Athens in Monroe (1887), has been rehabilitated and is held open by the Georgia Trust for Historic Preservation. Located at 319 McDaniels Street, Monroe; telephone: (706) 267-5602; call for an appointment 9:30-4:30; admission fee $2.00.

Augusta (Richmond County)

For information contact:
Historic Cotton Exchange Welcome Center, 32 Eighth Street, Augusta, Ga.
30901, telephone: (706) 724-4067, or (800) 726-0243.

SACRED HEART CULTURAL CENTER (1)

> 1301 Greene Street. Telephone: (706) 826-4700
> Open: Mon-Sat 10:00-4:00, Sun 1:00-4:00
> Admission fee $2.00
> Architects: Reverend Theodore Butler and Brother Cornelius Otten; based on the Sacred Heart
> Church, Galveston, TX, by Nicholas Clayton. Restoration by Spyro Meimarides
> Age: Built 1898-1900
> Style: Romanesque Revival

A lavish restoration effort in the mid-1980s culminated in the 1987 reopening of the former Catholic church as a center for community programs and for the arts. Sacred Heart's soaring interior is upstaged by the virtuoso display of the brickmason's craft on the exterior.

Brother Cornelius Otten, a Jesuit, moved about the Southeast helping to create and build outstanding churches. Sacred Heart is based on the design of Sacred Heart Church of Galveston, Texas, destroyed by a hurricane in 1900. Though Otten worked on the Texas church, Nicholas Clayton was the architect and Clayton claimed an architect's commission on the Augusta church due to its similarities with his original design. After leaving Augusta, Otten went on to design and build churches in Macon (Saint Joseph's Cathedral) and Tampa, Florida.

OLD MEDICAL COLLEGE OF GEORGIA (2)

> 598 Telfair Street. Telephone: (706) 724-4166
> Open Mon-Fri 10:00-5:00, Sat 9:00-12:00; guided tours available by appointment.
> No admission fee. Not handicapped accessible
> Architect: Charles B. Cluskey
> Age: Built in 1835
> Style: Greek Revival

Augusta's eminence in medical education and research can be traced to this building, which housed the first medical college in the state. After the medical school moved out, the building served a stint as a boys' military school. The Doric colonnade has a brooding presence on Telfair Street, but many of the interior

1. Sacred Heart Cultural Center
2. Old Medical College of Ga.
3. Ware's Folly
4. Broad St. Commercial Dist.
5. Old Town Victorian Neighborhood
6. St. Paul's Episcopal Church
7. Cotton Exchange
8. Church of the Good Shepherd
9. The Bon Air
10. Augusta National Golf Course

features have been stripped away over the years. It is now home to the Augusta Council of Garden Clubs and the Augusta Genealogical Society.

The architect of the Old Governor's Mansion in Milledgeville learned from his experience on this rotunda-design building. Cluskey almost found himself in a lawsuit over the building delays and cost overruns during construction. Contemporary architects should take heart: the roof has leaked since the day the building opened over 150 years ago.

WARE'S FOLLY (GERTRUDE HERBERT INSTITUTE OF ART) (3)

506 Telfair Street.
Telephone: (404) 722-5495
Open Tues-Fri 10:00-5:00, Sat
  10:00-2:00; closed in August
Adults $1.00, children, $ .50
Not handicapped accessible
Architect: Unknown, though the
  design has been attributed to both
  Daniel Pratt and Charleston
  architect Gabriel Manigault
Age: Built in 1818
Style: Federal

Ware's Folly

This mansion is known as Ware's Folly because Nicholas Ware spent the then almost unheard-of sum of $40,000 on its construction. It has been dedicated to the arts since it was saved from demolition in 1937 and now operates as a nonprofit art school and gallery.

Ware's Folly is one of the most delightful, lighthearted structures built during the Federal period. Stairs, doorways, and balconies all incorporate elliptical geometries. The effect is at once playful and dramatic. The craftsmanship is excellent for any period, but it is downright astonishing for what must be considered a frontier location at the time this house was built.

Nearby: BROAD STREET COMMERCIAL DISTRICT (4) has many fine mercantile brick and classical stone fronts. The unique, elevated Chamber of Commerce building (1977), in the center of the street, was designed by I. M. Pei & Associates.

OLD TOWN VICTORIAN NEIGHBORHOOD (5), east of Gordon Highway on Broad Street, is a gentrified Victorian district.

St. Paul's Episcopal Church (6)

605 Reynolds Street
Open Mon-Fri 9:00-5:00, Sat 10:00-1:00, and for Sun services
No admission fee. Partially handicapped accessible
Architect: Harry Wendell
Age: Built in 1919
Style: Neoclassical

This church is on the site of the original colonial fort built under the orders of James Oglethorpe, founder of the colony of Georgia. The fine Neoclassical interior of St. Paul's sanctuary is elliptically vaulted.

Nearby: The recently rehabilitated Cotton Exchange (7), 32 Eighth Street (rehabilitation by Virgil Gambill Rhoades, architects), anchors the ongoing Riverwalk project and provides excellent quarters for the Welcome Center.

Church of the Good Shepherd (8)

2230 Walton Way
Telephone: (706) 724-2485
Open for Sunday services
No admission fee
Architect: John J. Nesbit
Age: Built 1879-1880; burned
in 1896 and was rebuilt in 1898
with the original windows
Style: Gothic Revival

The Church of the Good Shepherd is a prime Georgia example of the type of architecture advocated by the famous nineteenth-century theorist John Ruskin. Color and decoration are not artificially applied to the surfaces of the building but arise naturally from the patterns, textures, and colors of the masonry, roofing, and woodwork. This approach to "permanent polychrome" has yielded a building that still looks as good as it did the day it was finished.

Church of the Good Shepherd

Nearby: The Church of the Good Shepherd is in the center of the Summerville Historic District, which is loosely bounded by Wrightsboro Road to the south, Highland Avenue to the west, Calhoun Expressway to the north, and Hickman Road to the east. The buildings date mostly from the1880s to the 1930s and embrace a stylistic mix of Gothic Revival, Queen Anne, Spanish Colonial, and others. The work of architect Lynn Drummond is an important contribution to Summerville's stock of fine homes. THE BON AIR (9), a large Neoclassical building housing the elderly, anchors the neighborhood at the corner of Walton and Hickman.

Summerville began as a summer resort for Augustans but became a year-round neighborhood. The Victorian era saw it become a winter resort for Northerners. Summerville's continued desirability as an intown neighborhood is surpassed in the state only by Atlanta's Buckhead community. Any time of year is pleasant for a driving or walking tour of Summerville. A tour of homes is held in late October.

The place that makes Augusta world famous one week a year, the AUGUSTA NATIONAL GOLF COURSE (10), is unfortunately not open to the public but can be glimpsed while driving by.

Washington (Wilkes County)

Washington is poised to enter the twenty-first century largely unchanged and certainly unimpressed by the twentieth. Far from being rundown and outmoded, this town has simply been choosy in allowing only those modernizations which can respectfully coexist with the area's deeply felt traditions.

History looms large here. Not only does the Civil War figure significantly in the area's history, but Wilkes County residents trace their ancestors back to a feisty band of Revolutionary War patriots that pushed the British back at the Battle of Kettle Creek and helped push them out of Augusta as well. The KETTLE CREEK BATTLEFIELD (not on map) can be seen 8 miles south of Washington on GA 44.

For information contact:
Washington-Wilkes Chamber of Commerce, 104 E. Liberty Street, P. O. Box 661, Washington, GA 30673, telephone (706) 678-2013.

WASHINGTON-WILKES HISTORICAL MUSEUM (1)

308 E. Robert Toombs Avenue. Telephone: (706) 678-2105
Open Tues-Sat 9:00-5:00, Sun 2:00-5:00

1. WASHINGTON-WILKES MUSEUM
2. ROBERT TOOMBS HOUSE
3. EPISCOPAL CHURCH OF THE MEDIATOR
4. WASHINGTON PRESBYTERIAN CHURCH
5. MARY WILLIS LIBRARY
6. FITZPATRICK HOTEL
7. CALLAWAY PLANTATION

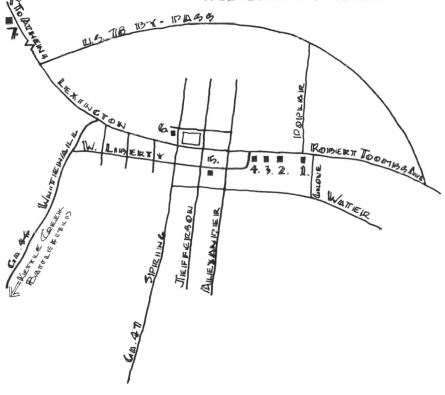

Admission fee $1.00. Not handicapped accessible
Architect: Restoration by Thomas G. Little and the Georgia Historical Commission
Age: Core is from about 1835; major additions date from 1856
Style: Federal Style with extensive additions

The first floor of this former residence is furnished in the period around the Civil War. Civil War (and later) memorabilia take up the second floor, while the basement contains a nice gallery of local history.

ROBERT TOOMBS HOUSE HISTORIC SITE (2)

216 E. Robert Toombs Avenue. Telephone: (706) 678-2226
Open Tues-Sat 10:00-5:00, Sun 2:00-5:00
Admission fee: $1.00. Partially handicapped accessible
Architect: Built by Dr. Joel Abbott
Age: Core of house dates from 1797. There have been many alterations including a Greek Revival front that dates from about 1850. Restoration efforts began in 1973.
Style: Greek Revival

Robert Toombs was Washington's flamboyant famous son whose apparent attraction to lost causes could have easily served as part of the role model for the character Rhett Butler in *Gone with the Wind*. Toombs, a wealthy lawyer and United States senator, tried to prevent the secession of the South from the Union. Soon, however, he became a member of the Confederate cabinet. This lasted until 1863, when he retired to Washington to begin bitterly criticizing the Confederate government. In a final twist, after the war he became a famous unreconstructed, unrepentant rebel who went into exile in France for some years. "I am not loyal to the existing government of the United States and do not wish to be suspected of loyalty," was one of his most memorable statements.

The house is much more interesting as a memorial to this eccentric character than it would be without his presence in its history. The most notable features are the furnished front rooms and the brick-floored basement room that housed his office.

Nearby: EPISCOPAL CHURCH OF THE MEDIATOR (3), Robert Toombs Avenue (1896), is a lovely, quaint shingle and clapboard building.

The sanctuary of the WASHINGTON PRESBYTERIAN CHURCH (4), Robert Toombs Avenue (1825), remains largely unchanged since its construction.

On Liberty Street at Jefferson stands the exuberant MARY WILLIS LIBRARY (5) (1888; Edmund Lind, architect; annex, 1977; Kuhkle & Wade, architects). The entry tower ingeniously transmogrifies as it rises from square to cylindrical to octagonal at the cap.

The FITZPATRICK HOTEL (6), 18 West Public Square (1897; Golucke &

Stewart, architects), is an interesting period piece in the Queen Anne style that has become a long-term rehabilitation project.

CALLAWAY PLANTATION (7)

US 78, 4 miles west of Washington
Open Tues-Sat 10-5, Sun 2-5 from April 15 to Dec 15 and during Christmas Season
Admission fee $1.00. Partially handicapped acccessible
Age: Built 1785-1869
Style: Greek Revival and others

The Callaway Plantation is both a working farm and a museum of buildings. The oldest structure is a hand-hewn log cabin dating from c. 1785. Also on the site are a two-story Plantation Plain style house named the Gilmer House and numerous outbuildings. The centerpiece is the 1869 brick Greek Revival plantation house, which has undergone the most complete restoration to nineteenth-century standards one can imagine, down to the candlelit rooms and outside toilets. Original plaster moldings and heart-pine floors are all intact. Many furnishings are original to the house. The Callaway Plantation is probably the most completely authentic example in the state of what a working nineteenth-century plantation looked and felt like.

Atlanta and Vicinity

Druid Hills and Emory (Dekalb County)

Designed by the nation's most famous landscape architect, Druid Hills is one of the state's most sublime works of landscape architecture. Frederick Law Olmstead was called to Atlanta in 1890 by Joel Hurt, who had purchased the Druid Hills tract for development. Olmstead's scheme dramatizes the rolling and occasionally steep terrain by creating a series of naturalistic parks in the ravines and hollows.

The residences overlooking the parks were designed by Georgia's premier architects of the period. Terrific romantic facades by Neel Reid, Philip Shutze, Hal Hentz, Henry Hornbostel, and Lewis Edmund Crook create an architectural backdrop unequaled in the state for artistry and congeniality both with each other and with their surroundings. The suburban ideal has reached a high point in Druid Hills.

Only one of the residences of Druid Hills is open to the public on a regular basis. Several houses, however, serve semipublic functions and can be counted on to be opened from time to time. A sampling of homes can be visited during the Druid Hills Home and Garden Tour held in early April. This tour is sponsored by the Atlanta Women's Chamber of Commerce.

CALLANWOLDE (1)

980 Briarcliff Road
Telephone: (404) 872-5338
Tours by appointment; open house hours are scheduled during the Christmas season; art gallery open Mon-Sat 10:00-3:00; administrative offices open Mon-Fri 9:00-5:30
Adults:$1.50, children $ .50
Architect: Henry Hornbostel
Age: Built in 1920
Style: Tudor

Callanwolde

The former home of Charles Howard Candler, this is now the Dekalb Fine Arts Center. The Christmas open house is a popular time to visit this grandly scaled residence.

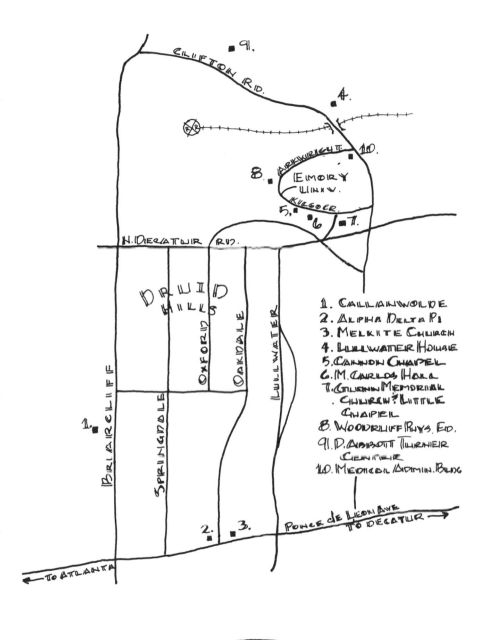

CLIFTON RD.

■ 9.

■ 4.

ARKWRIGHT

EMORY
UNIV.

■ 10.

8. ■

KILGOER

5. ■   ■ 6   ■ 7.

N. DECATUR RD.

DRUID
HILLS

BRIARCLIFF   SPRINGDALE   OXFORD   OAKDALE   LULLWATER

1. ■

1. CALLANWOLDE
2. ALPHA DELTA PI
3. MELKITE CHURCH
4. LULLWATER HOUSE
5. CANNON CHAPEL
6. M. CARLOS HALL
7. GLENN MEMORIAL
   CHURCH? LITTLE
   CHAPEL
8. WOODRUFF PHYS. ED.
9. P. ABBOTT TURNER
   CENTER
10. MEDICAL ADMIN. BLDG.

2. ■   ■ 3.

PONCE DE LEON AVE
TO DECATUR →

← TO ATLANTA

DRUID HILLS & EMORY
ATLANTA & VICINITY

Atlanta and Vicinity

Nearby: The first home occupied in Druid Hills (1910) is now the national headquarters of the **ALPHA DELTA PI SORORITY (2)**, 1386 Ponce de Leon Avenue; telephone: (404) 378-3164.

SAINT JOHN CHRYSOSTUM MELKITE CATHOLIC CHURCH (3), 1428 Ponce de Leon Avenue, was built as a one-story mansion by Asa Candler for his ailing wife. Much of the original interior has been altered over the years. The sanctuary nave was originally a sunken, glass-roofed atrium. The dining room was on a raised platform at the far end; telephone: (404) 373-9522.

LULLWATER HOUSE (4)

1463 Clifton Road
Open from time to time
for Emory University
functions. The house
has been featured on
the Druid Hills home
tour
Architects: Crook &
Ivey
Age: Built in 1926
Style: Tudor

Lullwater House

Lullwater House is architect Lewis Edmund Crook's masterpiece for Walter T. Candler, but its exquisite grounds almost upstage the architecture. It is now the home for the president of Emory University.

EMORY UNIVERSITY (5-10)

When Emory University left its campus near Covington for a suburban Atlanta location around 1915, architect Henry Hornbostel was hired to plan the new campus and design its first buildings. Hornbostel came up with a formal grouping of buildings, mostly two stories in height, faced with marble and stucco and roofed with clay tile.

Today's Emory has evolved into an uneasy coexistence between the original campus and the concrete behemoths inserted ever more densely into the already packed site. The only part of Hornbostel's plan left largely intact is the quadrangle, an oasis of serenity so far untouched by the jostling for space occurring just beyond its fringes. The Emory leadership has somewhat mitigated this problem by making a commitment to commissioning buildings of quality, often designed by internationally famous architects.

For information contact:
Emory University information, telephone (404) 727-6123.

CANNON CHAPEL (5)

Emory University Campus
Open Mon-Fri 7:30-4:30, for Sunday morning services at 11:15, and for scheduled events
No admission fee. Handicapped accessible
Architect: Paul Rudolph
Age: Built in 1980
Style: Modern

Cannon Chapel is one of the buildings on the fringe of the Emory Quadrangle. It is shoehorned into a site that appears better scaled for a kiosk than for a major campus building. Though quite Modernistic, the Chapel manages to respect the older buildings in massing and in roof material. In form the building is an imaginative pinwheel arrangement of stepping rectangular sections. It has no definite front; instead it is perceived more as a group of sculptural volumes topped with elliptically vaulted roofs.

MICHAEL CARLOS HALL (6)

On the Quadrangle of Emory University
Telephone: (404) 727-4282
Open Tues-Sat 11:00-4:30
Donation requested
Handicapped accessible
Architect: Henry Hornbostel; renovation
  by Michael Graves
Age: Completely renovated in 1985
Style: Postmodern

Formerly housing the law school, Carlos Hall has been rehabilitated into the university's Museum of Art and Archaeology. The 1985 redo designed by Michael Graves is a densely packed group of spaces with such presence that

Michael Carlos Hall

each could stand alone as the focus of the interior. Taken together, they create a pressurized container that is relieved only by the grand staircase and the light-hearted treatment of the upstairs lounge area. Don't miss the Graves-designed bathrooms.

Nearby: At the east Entrance to Emory stand GLENN MEMORIAL CHURCH (7) and the Education Building next door with its delightful LITTLE CHAPEL (1938-1939, both by Hentz, Adler & Shutze, architects). These works are based not on the Italian Baroque often associated with Shutze but on English Baroque ecclesiastic architecture. Glenn Memorial is open for performances as well as services. The Little Chapel, with its domed ceiling wholly enclosed by the Education Building, has its existence deliberately obscured from the exterior. The marvelous delicacy of its ornament in this 900-square-foot room is in keeping with its intimacy. Open Mon-Fri 9:00-4:00; no charge.

John Portman & Associates provided a welcome feeling of modesty by placing their immense state-of-the-art athletic center, the WOODRUFF PHYSICAL EDUCATION BUILDING (8), behind landscaped berms and by using the roof for tennis courts.

D. ABBOTT TURNER CENTER, CANDLER SCHOOL OF THEOLOGY (9)

855 Clifton Road
Telephone: (404) 727-8850
Open Mon-Fri 9:00-5:00; call for other hours; available for special programs
No admission fee
Handicapped accessible
Architects: Scogin, Elam & Bray
Age: Built in 1990
Style: Modern

D. Abbott Turner Center

The placement of the D. Abbott Turner Center behind an aging student housing complex on Clifton Road should not be taken as indication of modest intentions. This little building, brimming with ideas about space-making, challenges conventional forms and dashes preconceptions about building types. Tilted walls, swooping roof lines, and metal and glass enclose the offices, classrooms, and meeting space that make up the Center.

A ten-seat chapel at the rear of the building becomes a working garden folly: it is a small, highly wrought, attention-grabbing structure that focuses one's view on the landscape. Are such architectural gymnastics appropriate in a place of contemplation? Perhaps such a question says more about the viewer's preconceptions than about the architects' success in accomplishing their purpose.

Nearby: MEDICAL ADMINISTRATION BUILDING (10), Clifton Road at Arkwright. A Modernistic structure by Heery & Heery nicknamed "The Wedge," this building employs a dynamic geometry to good effect. Open Mon-Fri 9:00-5:00; no admission fee.

The Modern Movements

Eliminate ornament! Express function and materials! Use asymmetry and dynamic forms! Invoke the powerful image of the machine! These calls to action became the manifesto for one of architecture's most creative periods, a time when each new building takes a turn at answering the question: What does it mean to be "Modern"?

Because there is no one answer, Modernism has developed into a family of stylistic tendencies rather than a single mode of expression. As in any family, the members have often been estranged and severely critical of each other. Through the rancor, however, they continue to exhibit certain character traits that betray their origins.

The Modern family of styles includes Art Deco and its successor the Moderne (1920s-1930s), the International Style (1940s and 1950s), Late Modern (1960s to the present), High-Tech (1970s to the present), Postmodern (1970s and 1980s) and Deconstructivism (1980s to the present). Atlanta is well represented in modern architecture and is the place in Georgia to sample its many flavors.

Perhaps the most engaging of Modernism's tendencies, the Art Deco and Moderne styles are characterized by an optimistic countenance and an upbeat use of the latest materials of the day. Glass block, aluminum, stainless steel, and terrazzo were employed in these styles with much bravado. Traditional stone and brick were used in new ways to suggest streamlining rather than heaviness. Spring Street between Peachtree and North Avenue has a good collection of Moderne commercial buildings. Atlanta's best Art Deco exterior is on the AT&T building at 51 Peachtree Center Boulevard. Its limestone massing and low relief carvings are classic examples of Deco motifs.

The playfulness and optimism of the streamlined styles were replaced in the 1940s by the more austere International Style. This approach was born in prewar Germany out of the now clichéd yet persistent form-follows-function aesthetic. The style's emphasis on logic, rigor, and clarity made it the fully developed expression of Modernism and the ideological touchstone for all subsequent modern architecture. The library and the older College of Architecture building at Georgia Tech are leading local examples of this style. Its tenets became the basis for critical evaluation of buildings for decades to come, while at the same time its forced austerity became a constricting factor against artistic freedom.

Late Modern is well represented in Atlanta. In Late Modern, the compositional devices of the International Style remain intact, but the utilitarian connotations are eschewed in favor of the style's more voluptuous and sensual possibilities. The result is a less austere expression that creates more visual excitement and appeal for popular tastes. Luxurious materials such as granite, marble, brass, rare woods, and etched glass are employed along with dramatic spatial effects and elegant detailing to achieve this richer feeling. John Portman & Associates' Hyatt Regency and Peachtree Center Plaza hotels helped define this tendency for the nation, and other fine examples can be seen in most upscale Atlanta office parks and along Peachtree Street in Midtown.

High-Tech broke loose from the International Style's constraints by celebrating the mechanical and mechanistic aspects of modern life, employing a rich vocabulary of industrial colors, connections, and systems. A recent example of this aesthetic is the Callaway Manufacturing Research Center on the Georgia Tech Campus.

Deconstructivist works do not specifically reference the industrial aesthetic but instead incorporate modern steel and glass and such ordinary materials as corrugated plastic, galvanized sheet metal, and gypsum board in lively, tension-filled compositions that often seem to explode from the building's epicenter. Atlanta's few built examples of this relatively recent trend in architecture enjoy a high profile. Good representations of this tendency are the High Museum of Art by Richard Meier and Associates, Rio shopping center by Architectoniqua, and the Emory University's Candler School of Theology by Scogin, Elam & Bray.

A repudiation of Modernism for its shortcomings and a renewed appreciation of Classical and other traditional models of architecture formed the philosophical basis of Postmodernism. A Postmodern approach differs from outright traditionalism by not actually trying to recreate models of the past but instead attempting a blending or synthesis of traditional and modern elements. Michael Graves's Carlos Hall on the Emory University campus and his Hooker Development tower (now CocaCola) on 10th Street at W. Peachtree Street are delightful examples of Postmodernism in Atlanta.

Nothing ceases to excite the imagination more quickly than the widespread popularization of an idea. What began as an audacious paring of Modern and Classical concepts was soon seized by strip shopping center developers looking for eye-catching ways to draw in more customers. Despite being "stripped" of its ideology by being put extensively to such uses, Postmodernism provided a new vitality to mainstream architecture. A victim of its own success, it now fails to inspire the creative energy it did only a decade ago.

The style which began as a rejection of historicism has now become old enough to draw on its own history. This yet-to-be-named tendency has caught on quickly in Atlanta. Brought to the fore by the immense popular success of One Atlantic Center (the IBM tower) at 14th Street and W. Peachtree (John Burgee Architects with Philip Johnson), this "retro Modern" mode uses the latest technology to replicate the styles of the early twentieth-century skyscrapers. High profile buildings following this example have begun to appear at Lenox Square (Resurgens Plaza), Midtown (The Peachtree, Peachtree Street at 16th Street), and Downtown (191 Peachtree). The artistic basis for the trend seems to be primarily a draw on the welcome familiarity of the early skyscraper period's imagery. The resulting buildings are handsomely composed, convincingly detailed, and well-mannered. Creating buildings in this mode allows architects the pleasure of developing strong forms and rich decorative schemes without the problems of acceptance that a more avant-garde architecture might entail.

That Atlanta would be particularly receptive to a historicist approach should come as no surprise. Georgia's booming capital has a deep conservative streak and was a longtime holdout against widespread adoption of Modern architecture. A drive through its extensive suburbs reveals strong sympathies with traditional forms and a conservative distrust of stylistic innovation. And with few exceptions, Atlanta has not pioneered the building types or tendencies of Modernism.

Downtown and Midtown (Fulton County)

For information contact:
Atlanta Convention and Visitors Bureau,
233 Peachtree Street NE, Atlanta, GA 30303,
telephone (404) 521-6600. Branches are at
Lenox Square, Peachtree Center, and
Hartsfield International Airport.

HYATT REGENCY HOTEL (1)

265 Peachtree Street NE.
Telephone: (404) 577-1234
Always open
No admission fee. Handicapped accessible
Architect: John Portman & Associates
Age: Opened in 1967
Style: Modern

Hyatt Regency Hotel

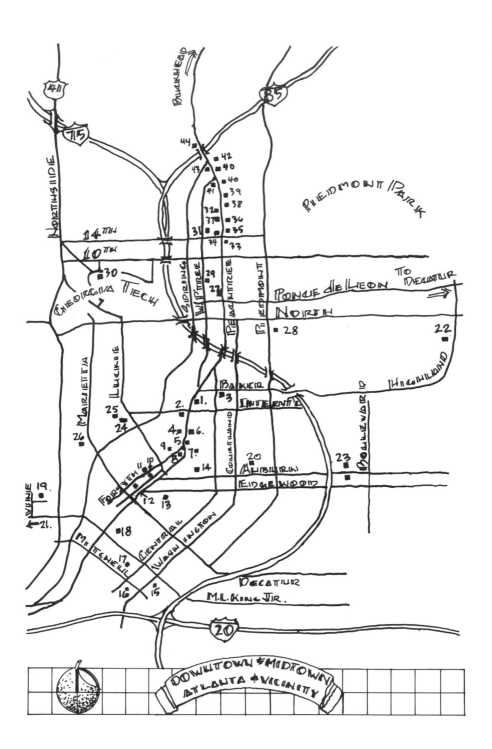

DOWNTOWN

1. Hyatt Regency
2. Peachtree Plaza
3. Marriott Marquis
4. Macy's
5. Peachtree Center MARTA Station
6. 191 Peachtree
7. Georgia-Pacific Center
8. Candler Building
9. Atlanta-Fulton County Library
10. Healey Building
11. Old Post Office
12. National Bank (C & S Bank)
13. Hurt Building
14. AT&T Communications Building
15. State Capitol
16. City Hall
17. Fulton County Government Center
18. Underground Atlanta
19. Herndon Home
20. Atlanta Life
21. Wren's Nest (off map)
22. Carter Presidential Center
23. Martin Luther King Jr. National Historic District
24. CNN Center
25. World Congress Center
26. Georgia Dome

MIDTOWN

27. Fox Theatre
28. Rio
29. Academy of Medicine
30. Callaway Manufacturing Research Center
31. One Atlantic Center
32. High Museum of Art
33. Campanile
34. Promenade
35. Colony Square
36. First Church of Christ Scientist
37. Atlanta Memorial Arts Center
38. Fulton County Public Library
39. Reid House
40. Federal Home Loan Bank
41. National Service Industries Building
42. Temple of the Hebrew Benevolent Congregation
43. Rhodes Hall
44. Brookwood Station

Atlanta and Vicinity

The Hyatt Regency, a breakthrough in modern architectural design, established John Portman's reputation. After 25 years, it still stands as one of the best atrium buildings ever conceived. The gee-whiz thrill of a visit to the Hyatt Regency has now been replaced by the more genteel, but still satisfying, pleasure of looking up an old friend who has done well for himself. The entry sequence to the atrium continues to delight, the fan-patterned tile floor is buffed and shiny, the glitzy elevator cars still glide quietly, and the Polaris Lounge turns slowly overhead. It matters little that what was once a landmark on Atlanta's skyline has now been eclipsed by its taller and newer neighbors.

Nearby: PEACHTREE PLAZA HOTEL (2), Peachtree Street at International Boulevard, was also designed by John Portman & Associates (1974). This slick gray cylinder is still the tallest hotel in the world.

MARRIOTT MARQUIS HOTEL (3)

265 Peachtree Center Avenue. Telephone: (404) 521-0000
Always open
No admission fee. Handicapped accessible
Architect: John Portman & Associates
Age: Built 1984
Style: Modern

The interior of the Marriott Marquis brings to mind how Jonah may have felt inside the whale. Portman & Associates reinvigorated the now humdrum hotel atrium concept with a building baroque in its manipulation of space but restrained in its detailing and finishes. Impressive engineering and design skill are evidenced in the creation of a tower in which each floor is a slightly different shape.

MACY'S (4)

180 Peachtree Street NW. Telephone: (404) 221-7221
Open Mon-Sat; call for hours
No admission fee. Handicapped accessible
Architects: Hentz, Adler & Shutze, with Starrett & Van Vleet (New York)
Age: Built in 1927
Style: Neoclassical

Atlanta's last major downtown department store is also its best. The main floor is generously proportioned and is modulated by pier-like columns with leafy gold capitals. The dignified exterior, rendered in limestone and brick, features generous openings and a heavy cornice.

PEACHTREE CENTER MARTA STATION (5)

Entrances along Peachtree Street. Telephone: (404) 848-4711
Open when MARTA is running, most days until 11:00 PM
Fare $1.00. Handicapped accessible
Architects: Toombs, Amisano & Wells
Age: Built in 1980

MARTA has made a concerted effort to integrate art into all its stations, but only at Peachtree Center does the station become art. The juxtaposition of sleek rapid-transit cars whooshing past high-tech platforms against the tunnel walls of the exposed granite of Peachtree ridge reveals the Modern sensibility at its best. The long escalator ride down (not for the acrophobe) helps set the mood for this meditation on the continuum between the new and the primeval.

Nearby: The skyscraper named **191 PEACHTREE** (**6**) is the younger cousin of midtown's ONE ATLANTIC CENTER (**31**) (both by John Burgee Architects with Philip Johnson). The newer building presents a sophisticated and engaging entrance that abuts the sidewalk rather than being placed behind a breezy plaza like so many downtown towers. Inside, colossal chandeliers hang over granite floors, black marble trim, and travertine covered walls that look like big, luscious blocks of cream cheese. If you've been considering a marble crypt for your last resting place, try one of this building's elevators on for size.

GEORGIA-PACIFIC CENTER (7)

133 Peachtree Street NE, at Margaret Mitchell Square. Telephone: (404) 521-4000
Open Mon-Fri 9:00-5:00
No admission fee. Handicapped accessible
Architects: Skidmore Owings Merrill
Age: Built in 1982
Style: Modern

The Georgia-Pacific tower helped reignite downtown as a location for major building projects. Designed as the tallest building in the Southeast, it is cleanly detailed and enjoys an easily identified stepped silhouette. The design relies on these two elements too exclusively, however, to live fully up to its potential as the South's flagship building. The best thing to happen here in recent years is the incorporation of the small High Museum annex tucked into some leftover space on the lower floors (1986; Scogin, Elam and Bray, architects). The architects added some intrigue and density to the otherwise staightforward tower by treating the museum annex as a bulding within a building. The effect created by its vaulted interior roof, ramps, slate floors, and precise carpentry is that of an elegant handcrafted submarine that has somehow docked inside the building.

121

Atlanta and Vicinity

CANDLER BULDING (8)

127 Peachtree Street
Telephone: (404) 523-
1200
Open Mon-Fri 9:00-
5:00
No admission fee
Handicapped accessible
Architect: Murphy &
Stewart
Age: Built in 1906
Style: Neoclassical

Candler Building

This grande dame of Atlanta office buildings is aging magnificently with the help of a recent, skillfully executed facelift. The marble and terra cotta exterior is ennobled at the entrances with F. B. Miles's famous sculptures. Though modestly scaled by modern standards, the marble-clad lobby exhibits a panache that reveals just how overblown many recent office building lobbies have become.

Nearby: The ATLANTA-FULTON PUBLIC LIBRARY (9), 1 Margaret Mitchell Square SW, one of Marcel Breuer's last works, is so sculpturally striking that the banality of its interiors comes as a letdown. Breuer, who is also known for designing the Whitney Museum in New York and the famous chair that bears his name, seemed more at home dealing with objects than with spaces. Telephone: (404) 688-4636; call for hours; no admission fee; handicapped accessible.

HEALEY BUILDING (10)

57 Forsyth Street NW. Telephone: (404) 522-3147
Open Mon-Fri 9:00-5:00
No admission fee. Handicapped accessible
Architects: Morgan & Dillon with W. T. Downing; historic rehabilitation by Stang & Newdow
Age: Built in 1913
Style: Gothic Revival

The quip that developers never have enough money to do the job right but always have enough to do it again was reversed in the case of the Healey Building. A planned second tower for this mixed-use project was never constructed, but what was built was done well. One of Atlanta's grand pre-Modern office buildings, the Healey building is distinguished by its Gothic Revival style. Gothic stone ribbing gives verticality and scale to the exterior and a church-like gravity to the interior. Ornate mailboxes and other inventive details help liven up what might have otherwise been too solemn for a place of commerce.

A welcome civic-mindedness prevails in the ground-floor lobby/pedestrian mall. The mid-block rotunda is a remarkable space that would have been the connecting element had the second tower been built. Atlanta is fortunate that, given the devil's choice between doing it right or doing it again, the original owners of the Healey Building took the higher road.

Nearby: Across Forsyth Street the OLD POST OFFICE (11) building epitomizes what used to be called "a grand pile," meaning an impressive pile of masonry. This pallazzo (Italian palace) for the US Government has been recently renovated for the Circuit Court of Appeals. Designed by John Knox Taylor and completed in 1911, the building is not open to the touring public, but visitors can enjoy a quick peek inside before being asked to leave.

NATIONSBANK (FORMERLY C & S BANK) (12)

> 35 Broad Street NW. Telephone: (404) 581-5083
> Open Mon-Fri 9:00-4:00
> No admission fee. Partially handicapped accessible
> Architects: Morgan & Dillon; renovation by Philip Shutze (Hentz, Adler & Shutze)
> Age: Originally built in 1901; Shutze addition in 1929
> Style: Neoclassical

Philip Shutze's renovation of the Empire Building's lower three floors resulted in the architect's most famed interior. The grand banking hall is based primarily on the motifs of the Pantheon in Rome. Shutze's achievement is a space utterly convincing in the authority of its design and thoroughly satisfying in the precision of its execution. Rooms like this make the most compelling argument for a return to Classicism.

HURT BUILDING (13)

> 45 Edgewood Avenue SE. Telephone: (404) 522-3888
> Open Mon-Fri 9:00-5:00
> No admission fee. Handicapped accessible
> Architect: J. E. R. Carpenter, New York; rehabilitation by Associated Space Design
> Age: Completed in 1924; rehabilitation in 1985

When it reopened, the seventeen-story Hurt Building became downtown's most lauded historic rehabilitation project. The rotunda entrance, imbued with Neoclassical grandeur, and an upstairs restaurant make good use of the architectural features.

Nearby: AT&T COMMUNICATIONS BUILDING **(14)**, 51 Peachtree Center Avenue (1922-1929; Marye, Alger & Venour, architects), has downtown's best Art Deco facades. The heroic and highly ornate entrance, however, leads to a disappointingly plain, small lobby. The building you see was to have been the base for a skyscraper that was never built.

STATE CAPITOL (15)

206 Washington Street
Security Office Telephone: (404) 656-3277
Open Mon-Fri 8:30-5:30
No admission fee (security check required)
Handicapped accessible
Architects: Edbrooke & Burnham, Chicago
Age: Built in 1889
Style: Neoclassical

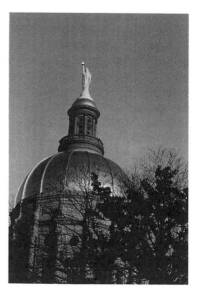

With its superb siting, well-composed facades, and handsomely proportioned dome, Georgia's State Capitol is an imposing and satisfying landmark. The interior contains some dwarfing multileveled spaces but is finished plainly (some marble wainscot here, a Corinthian column there) and does not appear opulent. It has changed little since its construction and is now so full of state memorabilia that it feels more like a museum than the headquarters of one of the nation's fastest growing states.

State Capitol

CITY HALL (16)

68 Mitchell Street SW. Telephone: (404) 658-6000
Open Mon-Fri 8:30-5:30
No admission fee. Handicapped accessible
Architect: G. Lloyd Preacher; 1989 addition and renovations by Muldawer & Moultrie/ Jova
 Daniels Busby/ Harris & Partners
Age: Built in 1930
Style: Gothic Revival

See the discussion of City Hall under FULTON COUNTY GOVERNMENT CENTER below.

FULTON COUNTY GOVERNMENT CENTER (17)

Pryor Street between Martin Luther King Jr. Drive and Mitchell Street
Open Mon-Fri 8:30-5:30
No admission fee. Handicapped accessible
Architects: Rosser-Fabrap International/Turner & Associates
Style: Modern

The architects of Atlanta's City Hall employed every means possible to distinguish it from the State Capitol, which is diagonally across the street. Rather than a sprawling masonry mass based on Classical antiquity, City Hall is a seventeen-story Gothic Revival tower rendered primarily in light terra cotta tiles. Setbacks in the tower and an observatory further enhance its verticality over the Capitol's predominant horizontal lines. The lobby is a compact space befitting a city too busy hustling for growth to worry over pomp.

The 1989 addition speaks of an entirely different Atlanta and should be seen in contrast with the even newer Fulton County Government Center. Both buildings are centered on greenhouse-roofed atriums and both make big statements about a city that enjoyed spectacular prosperity during the 1980s. The similar time frames, uses, and spatial organization, but different intentions that went into making these buildings provides a unique opportunity for comparison.

The new addition to City Hall employs green mirror glass and precast concrete to reflect and amplify the details of the original building. Inside, the atrium's multicolored marble flooring and center fountain enliven this dignified and important looking but ultimately vacant space. The new Fulton County Government Center, connected by a bridge across Pryor Street to the original Fulton County building, makes no effort to be anything but Modern. Granite is used here as the major character-giving material. The atrium is not a contained, quiet space but rather a kinetic composition that spills (literally, with an outdoor waterfall) out to the street and engages passersby. Terraces, mezzanines, pavilions, and palm trees enliven the atrium, which is used by visitors and employees. The Fulton County Center even has a food court.

Should our government be conducted in quiet, dignified surroundings, or should it compete with malls and office buildings to draw people in? How should government buildings reflect a region's prosperity and growing world prominence? How should they address the urban street life around them? How ingratiating should their appearance be to neighboring historic buildings? City Hall and the Fulton County Government Center address these fundamental architectural issues with remarkable clarity and completely different answers.

UNDERGROUND ATLANTA (18)

Area bounded roughly by Peachtree, Pryor, and Alabama Streets and Martin Luther King Jr. Boulevard. Telephone: (404) 586-2396
Open Mon-Sun; various businesses keep different hours
No admission fee. Handicapped accessible
Architects: Cooper Carry & Associates with Turner Associates were the primary architects for the area's rehabilitation.

A national survey revealed that Underground was visitors' favorite destination in Atlanta. Remarkably, this news came several years after the entertainment center had closed. The survey became the impetus for Underground's reopening in 1990 as a Rouse Company development.

The new Underground is not so much an architectural statement as it is an urban theme park. Unlike the Disney ersatz ver-

Light Tower, Underground Atlanta

sions, however, this park is the real thing knit into a real city, and it provides a different sort of satisfaction. As the name implies, a significant portion of the complex is under the street grid. The old-looking building facades are geniune; they date primarily from the late nineteenth century.

Though the light tower and fountain plaza do provide a focus, it is impossible to summarize Underground in a single scene or photograph. It is often times such details as the lamp posts and other street furniture, and the transition from large spaces to intimate ones or from old to new buildings, that create the most memorable impressions. Underground doesn't try to leave the visitor in awe; it issues an invitation to return and poke around some more.

The Coca-Cola Museum (1990; Thompson, Ventulett and Stainback, architects) is part of the Underground Atlanta complex. The sixteenth-century Italian architect Andrea Palladio stressed that architecture should provide "commodity, firmness and delight." The Coca-Cola Museum may be shy on the first two qualities, but it provides so much delight that it doesn't matter. From the continuous Coca-Cola logo frieze to the glass corner column to the kinetic entry plaza, this building is about humor and fun. To criticize it for lacking substance would be like criticizing an ice cream cone for lacking nutritional balance. Open Mon-Sat 10:00-9:30, Sun 12:00-6:00; handicapped accessible.

HERNDON HOME (19)

587 University Place. Telephone: (404) 581-9813
Open Tues-Sat 10:00-4:00; tours start on the hour
No admission fee. Not handicapped accessible
Age: Built in 1910
Style: Neoclassical

Designed not by a trained architect but by Alonzo Herndon's wife Adrienne, this house exhibits spatial ingenuity, elegant detail, and fine craftsmanship. Though Mrs. Herndon tragically died as the house was nearing completion, it was enjoyed for many years by her spouse and by their son Norris.

Starting off life as a slave, Alonzo Herndon made himself into one of the nation's foremost black businessmen. He sited his house with a commanding view over Atlanta. Its ironspot brick facades, with elliptically arched first-floor openings and giant fluted columns defining the front porch, create a sense of both stability and defiance that seems an apt reflection of its original owner. Inside the mahogany-panelled den and dining room are elegant spaces that remain unchanged since Norris Herndon died, leaving the house to the Herndon Foundation to be preserved for the public.

Today the house is kept open proudly by the Herndon Foundation at no charge to visitors. The spirit imbued in the house will be ever more needed as the precincts of the new Georgia Dome, a gigantic covered sports arena, creep up to its doorstep. Somehow there seems to be little need to worry that the Herndon Home will continue to persevere through these next challenges.

Nearby: ATLANTA LIFE INSURANCE (20), 100 Auburn Avenue, is the largest enterprise founded by Alonzo Herndon. It is one of downtown Atlanta's little gems—a model of crisp modern design (Thompson, Ventulett & Stainback, architects).

WREN'S NEST (21), 1050 Gordon Street, is the former home of Joel Chandler Harris. Harris had this cottage remodeled into a Queen Anne style confection but left the interiors quite plain. Telephone: (404) 753-7735; open Tues-Sat 10:00-5:00, Sun 2:00-5:00; adults $3.00; not handicapped accessible.

CARTER PRESIDENTIAL CENTER (22)

1 Copen Hill Avenue. Telephone: (404) 331-0296
Open Mon-Sat 9:00-4:45, Sun 12:00-4:45
Adults $2.50, seniors $1.50, under 16 free. Handicapped accessible
Architects: Jova Daniels Busby
Style: Modern

Atlanta and Vicinity

Sometimes distinctive architecture becomes a tourist attraction, but rarely does a planned tourist attraction aim for serious architectural interest. The Carter Presidential Center has successfully hit both targets. Designed to accommodate conferences, offices, and a visitors' center that traces Jimmy Carter's days in the presidency, the Carter Presidential Center has become an important stop on any Atlanta sightseeing tour. The building is in plan a set of interlocking round pavilions. Its execution cuts neatly between staid government building and entertainment architecture. A formal contemporary colonnade leads to the entrance in the center pavilion. The entry hall is an unexpectedly generous, freely flowing space which opens up to the galleries, garden, eating area, and administrative area.

Nearby: Atlanta's role as the birthplace of civil rights is aptly documented in the MARTIN LUTHER KING JR. HISTORIC DISTRICT (23) (Auburn Avenue between Courtland Street and Boulevard). The district is administered and developed under the National Park Service and features King's boyhood home, Ebeneezer Baptist Church, and the King Center for Social Change.

CNN CENTER (24)

1050 Techwood Drive NW. Telephone: (404) 827-2491
Open every day
No admission fee. Handicapped accessible
Architects: Thompson, Ventulett & Stainback
Age: Opened in 1975
Style: Modern

CNN Center was named The Omni until Ted Turner's organization became its signature tenant in 1986. This project launched the career one of Atlanta's most venerable architectural firms.

Megastructures like CNN Center are fundamentally different in concept from atrium buildings such as the Hyatt Regency. The atrium is a large space carved out of a building's center. The megastructure is conceived as a group of buildings that have roofed and air-conditioned the space between them. While both focus inward, the megastructure is executed at a much bigger scale; it affects to be a city in miniature.

Though megastructures were initially seen as an exciting new development in Modern architecture, urban designers were quick to characterize them as architectural godzillas chewing up huge parcels of urban land. If entire cities were redeveloped in this way, they pointed out, street life would cease to exist. This criticism, however, probably had little to do with the decline of the building type. The economics of creating so much space in one effort makes profitability a difficult proposition. CNN Center is no exception; it has lost a lot of money for a lot of people. As a result, architects and developers have returned to creating cities the old fashioned way—one piece at a time.

CNN Center today is simultaneously a tourist attraction, a work of architecture on a grand scale, and a part of recent architectural history. The ice rink and glamorous boutiques originally housed in the Center have been replaced by prosaic shops and more eating establishments. The limestone, glass, and precast building facades, though well composed, are secondary in importance to the cathedralesque interior. This vast space reminds us of a day when the development business was more freewheeling and architects wanted to remold their cities with large gestures. The "megalithic" period has come and gone; Atlanta is not likely to see any more of these great beasts lumbering into town.

Nearby: WORLD CONGRESS CENTER (25), next door to CNN Center (Thompson, Ventulett & Stainback, architects), is the gigantic exhibition hall where Atlanta conventioneers spend most of their time. The GEORGIA DOME (26) (Thompson Ventulett & Stainback, Heery International, and Rosser Fabrap joint venture architects), just behind the World Congress Center, is the state's largest indoor space. It is open for sporting and other events.

FOX THEATER (27)

600 Peachtree Street NE. Telephone: (404) 881-1977
Open for performances and private parties
Admission fee varies. Partially handicapped accessible
Architects: Marye, Algour & Vinour
Age: Built in 1929
Style: Moorish Revival

"Save the Fox!" was Atlanta's preservation cry during the 1970s. The thought that anyone could even consider tearing down Atlanta's most venerable architectural landmark is still chilling a decade after its rescue by the Save the Fox Foundation.

Only a rare building can steadfastly refuse to operate at a profit for its owners for more than 60 years and still survive. This masonry and steel femme fatale has been charming successive owners into its labor of love since it opened prophetically in 1929, shortly after the stock market crash, and closed for the first time in 1932. The Fox has hosted several grand reopenings since. Its threatened demolition by Southern Bell finally galvanized the preservation community in a town that ordinarily dislikes looking back.

The Fabulous Fox is one of those buildings inevitably described with superlatives. Its exterior is a city block of striped masonry, Moorish arches, and onion domes that create a suggestive veil for the pleasures within. Once inside the 3000-seat theater, the visitor feels he has stepped outside into an Islamic courtyard. The sun goes down, clouds drift by, and the stars come out just in time for the show to begin. Fantasy never descends to hokum at the Fox; its execution and level of detail are captivating. The bathrooms alone would be the high point in most buildings. To those of us inured to the impoverished environments of shopping center movie houses, a trip to the Fabulous Fox is a reminder that the theater itself can be part of the performance.

Nearby: RIO **(28)**, a shopping center at 179 North Avenue, at the corner of Piedmont Avenue (1989; Architectoniqua, architects), opened with much fanfare as a brash concept merging entertainment with shopping. It failed to catch on and now is something of a ghost town.

ACADEMY OF MEDICINE **(29)**, 875 West Peachtree Street (1941; R. Kennon Perry with Hentz, Adler & Shutze, architects), is a Regency style building. The sureness of its interior composition reveals the talented hand of Philip Shutze. The Academy is currently in better shape than ever before thanks to its restoration by Surber Barber Mooney, architects. Telephone: (404) 881-1714. It is available for special occasions.

FULLER CALLAWAY MANUFACTURING RESEARCH CENTER **(30)**, on the Georgia Tech Campus (1991; Lord, Aeck & Sargent, architects), reinvigorates the High-Tech aesthetic with such inventive details as cog-volute column capitals and spiral staircases that appear ready to auger into the foundation.

ONE ATLANTIC CENTER (IBM TOWER) (31)

West Peachtree at 14th Street. Telephone: (404) 877-4000
Open Mon-Fri 9:00-5:00
No admission fee. Handicapped accessible
Architects: John Burgee Architects with Philip Johnson, New York
Age: Built in 1987

The IBM Tower has enjoyed tremendous critical and popular success in Atlanta. Its Gothic detailing deliberately recalls the New York skyscrapers of the early twentieth century. The pink granite exterior culminates in a distinctive pyramidal cap, handsomely lit at night. Its strong silhouette and the welcome familiarity generated by its traditional-looking facades have influenced the design of an entire generation of Atlanta towers. The lobby design unabashedly revels in marble opulence. It leads to an extensively landscaped but seldom used plaza on West Peachtree Street.

HIGH MUSEUM OF ART (32)

1280 Peachtree Street.
Telephone: (404) 892-3600
Open Tues-Thur and Sat 10:00-5:00,   Fri 10:00-9:00, Sun 12:00-5:00

Adults $4.00, students and senior
citizens $2.00
Handicapped accessible
Architect: Richard Meier &
Associates
Age: Built in 1983
Style: Modern

Meier took a white box, elegantly exploded one corner, and carefully composed the pieces strewn across the lawn. The resulting building exists in exquisite tension between chaos and order. The High Museum is much more than a container for artwork: it seems to interact with whatever is placed inside. Its reputation quickly spread, and now it is often mentioned as one of the best buildings built in America in the 1980s.

A WALKING TOUR OF MIDTOWN
BEGINNING AT 14TH STREET AND
HEADING NORTH (33-44)

High Museum of Art

The High Museum gives focus to Midtown. This is the one section of the city that actually achieves the image of genteel urbanity that Atlanta has set as a goal for itself. The roughly ten-block-long stretch of Peachtree contains some of the city's most sophisticated architecture. Generously landscaped setbacks from the street create a parkway effect not present in the hard-surfaced Central Business District. An agreeable mix of cultural, religious, and commercial buildings makes for a chic yet relaxed setting for the street life. As real estate prices in the area soar, this favorable situation is likely to change for the worse.

CAMPANILE (33) (Southern Bell Tower), SE corner of Peachtree Street at 14th Street (1987), was designed by Thompson Ventulett & Stainback, architects. Lobby is open Mon-Fri 9:00-5:00. No admission fee; handicapped accessible.

PROMENADE (34), NW corner of Peachtree Street at 14th (1978-1991), is a building complex for AT&T (Thompson Ventulett & Stainback, Ai Group architects). Lobby open Mon-Fri 9:00-5:00; No admission fee; handicapped accessible.

COLONY SQUARE (35), 1175 Peachtree Street (1970; Jova Daniels Busby, architects; several alterations of interior since then by others), NE corner at 14th. One of two megastructures in Atlanta, Colony Square trailblazed commercial redevelopment in this area. Open seven days a week 8:00-6:00; some restaurants and the hotel keep later hours. No admission fee; handicapped accessible.

FIRST CHURCH OF CHRIST SCIENTIST (36), NE corner of Peachtree at 15th (1914; Edward Doughtery & Arthur Neal Robinson, architects). This impressive Neoclassical building is holding its own against the much taller office buildings springing up around it. Open for Sunday services; no admission fee.

ATLANTA MEMORIAL ARTS CENTER (37), 1280 Peachtree Street NW (Toombs Amisano & Wells with Stevens & Wilkinson, architects), corner at 15th. The Arts Center, including the High Museum, is now a two-building complex. The older building to the south houses the Atlanta Symphony and the Alliance Theater. Box Office Telephone: (404) 892-2414; no charge to enter lobby; handicapped accessible.

FULTON COUNTY PUBLIC LIBRARY (38), Peachtree Branch, 1315 Peachtree Street (1987; Thompson Ventulett & Stainback, architects), presents a stepped-glass facade to Peachtree. Telephone: (404) 872-8630; no admission fee; handicapped accessible.

REID HOUSE (39), 1325 Peachtree Street NE (1924; Hentz, Reid & Adler, architects with Philip Shutze), is a handsome Neoclassical private apartment building. Not open to the public.

FEDERAL HOME LOAN BANK BUILDING (40), 1475 Peachtree Street (Smallwood Reynolds Stewart & Stewart, architects), is a Modern, red granite-clad building with a curved front and cascading fountains. Open Mon-Fri 9:00-5:00; no admission fee; handicapped accessible.

NATIONAL SERVICE INDUSTRIES BUILDING (41), Peachtree Street at West Peachtree (1990; Cooper Carry & Associates, architects). A wedge shape design exploits the building's location at Pershing Point. No admission fee; handicapped accessible.

TEMPLE OF THE HEBREW BENEVOLENT CONGREGATION (42), 1589 Peachtree Street NE (1929; Hentz, Adler & Shutze, architects), is in the Neoclassical style.

RHODES HALL (43), 1516 Peachtree Street (1904; W. F. Denney, architect). This Romanesque Revival stone mansion is now the home of the Georgia Trust for Historic Preservation, which provides regular tours. It is a wonderful example of the

Rhodes Hall

Victorian Romanesque. Telephone: (404) 881-9980; open Mon-Fri 11:00-4:00; admission fee $2.00; not handicapped accessible.

BROOKWOOD STATION (44), 1688 Peachtree Street (1918; Hentz Reid and Adler, architects with Philip Shutze). This Neoclassical jewel box was once Atlanta's suburban train station. Now it is Atlanta's *only* train station.

The North Side (Fulton and Cobb Counties)

Most large cities seem to wish they were flat, if we can judge by the way they relentlessly extend an orthogonal street grid in every direction. Atlanta delights in revealing its topographical dimension. Street grids never extend far before being interrupted. Peachtree Street's bends and curves trace Atlanta's central ridge formation. This feature is most easily seen from I-20 at the top of the hill in Douglasville. The city's linear character becomes clear as virtually all of its buildings of any pretension toe up to Peachtree like players on a line of scrimmage.

Nowhere is the lay of the area's terrain more perfectly exploited than in the residential section of Buckhead. Houses on Habersham, West Paces Ferry, Andrews, Peachtree Battle, and other roads benefit from placement guided almost exclusively by aesthetics. Narrow roadways wind through the gentlest contours, while the houses sit regally on the flanking hillsides. Tudor mansions, Italian villas, Federal homes, and the occasional Modernistic design coexist gracefully on spacious sloping lawns and under canopies of mature hardwoods. Buckhead houses are rarely opened to the public; a drive by is typically all the visitor can enjoy. SWAN HOUSE (1) is an exception.

SWAN HOUSE (1)

3101 Andrews Drive NW. Telephone: (404) 261-1837
Open Mon-Sat 9:00-5:30, Sun 12:00-5:30
Adults $6.00. Handicapped accessible
Architects: Hentz, Adler & Shutze
Age: Completed in 1930
Style: Italian Villa

Only someone who studied the classics well, knew them intimately, and was sure of his artistry could reinterpret the Italian villa with such effect as Philip Shutze did in the Swan House, designed for Mr. and Mrs. Edward Inman and now part of the Atlanta Historical Society complex. Shutze, like William Jay a century earlier, was so far ahead of the pack that he truly had no contemporaries. The

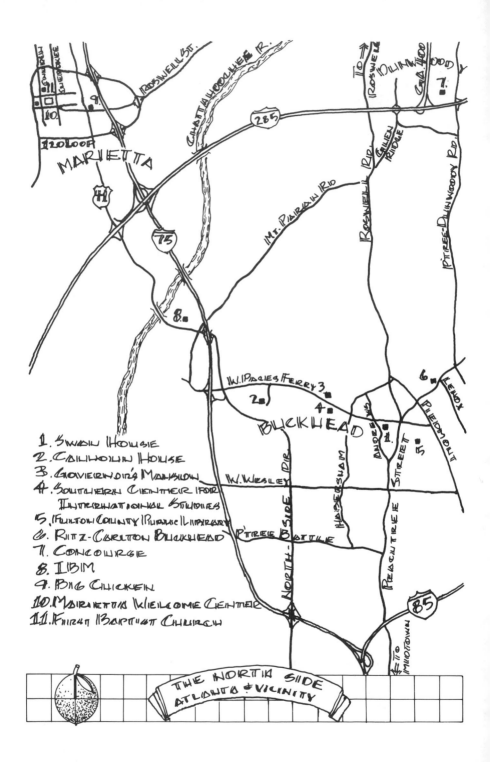

1. SWAN HOUSE
2. CALHOUN HOUSE
3. GOVERNOR'S MANSION
4. SOUTHERN CENTER FOR
   INTERNATIONAL STUDIES
5. FULTON COUNTY PUBLIC LIBRARY
6. RITZ-CARLTON BUCKHEAD
7. CONCOURSE
8. IBM
9. BIG CHICKEN
10. MARIETTA WELCOME CENTER
11. FIRST BAPTIST CHURCH

THE NORTH SIDE
ATLANTA & VICINITY

Swan House

powerful expression he could create out of the elements of Classicism was inimitable. Shutze understood proper siting, good composition, and taste, but these qualities alone would not lift the Swan House to its triumph. Only the architect's sure grasp of the Classical's potential could make the Swan House both a lesson in the emotional power inherent in Classicism and an artifact of beauty. In other works, Shutze composed designs to achieve an expression of lightheartedness, melancholy, delicacy, gravity, urbanity, the country life, and much more. At the Swan House, Shutze's street facade displays a lighthearted, feminine composition with playful curves and delicately undulating features. The entry (rear) facade's Doric portico and straight lines are somber and masculine.

The interior composition freely combines and plays off the two moods introduced on the facades. The geometry of the circular entrance hall is embellished upon in the design of the spiraling stair in the next room. On either side, rooms of decidedly masculine or feminine character alternate. Shutze's career and the Swan House are both well documented for those who want to know more. The Swan house is a state treasure.

Nearby: The pillars at the corner of West Paces Ferry and Pinestream were once the gateway for the CALHOUN HOUSE (2) (private), another Shutze masterpiece, but now form the entrance to a subdivision surrounding the home.

The GOVERNOR'S MANSION (3), 391 West Paces Ferry Road, offers tours of its first floor. Telephone: (404) 261-1776; open Tues-Thurs 10:00-11:30.

The SOUTHERN CENTER FOR INTERNATIONAL STUDIES (4), 320 West Paces Ferry Road, is another Shutze-designed house that is occasionally open for visitors. Telephone: (404) 261-5763.

The Buckhead branch of the FULTON COUNTY PUBLIC LIBRARY (5), 269 Buckhead Avenue, exemplifies the kinetic work of Scogin, Elam & Bray. Telephone: (404) 233-2108.

The Lenox Square area boasts a rapidly changing skyline. Here the RITZ-CARLTON BUCKHEAD (6), Peachtree Road at Lenox Road (Smallwood Reynolds Stewart & Stewart, architects), offers variety to Atlanta's reputation as a great hotel town by reinterpreting the European model of elegance.

CONCOURSE (7)

Peachtree-Dunwoody Boulevard at I-285
Office buildings open Mon-Fri 9:00-5:00;
the Doubletree Hotel is always open
No admission fee. Handicapped accessible
Architects: Thompson, Ventulett &
Stainback
Age: Built in the 1980s
Style: Modern

Concourse

To create architecture on the scale of a small city is both a glamorous and a challenging task. In office park design, issues customarily addressed by city planning or laissez-faire urban growth are given architectural solutions. Most office parks try for a landscape concept in which the buildings are isolated structures in a park setting. This scheme keeps the project from looking unfinished if not all the planned buildings are constructed, but it often ignores the potential for interesting spaces between buildings.

The Concourse plan reverses the usual figure-ground relationship by enclosing a significant outdoor space, in this case a lake. The lake becomes in effect the project's town square. Ironically, in this urban concept the buildings become more a background element than they do in the landscape solution. Here the urban outdoor space becomes the central element, and the structures perform a facilitating role. A steady building program during the 1980s has given Concourse a finished appearance rare for a suburban office park.

Nearby: The **DUNWOODY** neighborhood is Atlanta's most prestigious suburban office park area. Buildings designed by Kevin Roche, Welton Beckett, and other well-known firms dot the landscape.

ROSWELL (not on map), in north Fulton County, is a historic town with a walking tour and buildings open to the public.

For information contact:
Roswell Historical Society, 227 South Atlanta Street, Roswell, GA 30075; telephone (404) 992-1665.

IBM SOUTHWEST MARKETING HEADQUARTERS (8)

4111 Northside Parkway
Telephone: (404) 238-2000
Open Mon-Fri 9:00-5:00
No admission fee. Handicapped accessible
Architects: Thompson, Ventulett & Stainback
Style: Modern

*IBM Southwest Marketing
Headquarters*

Ordinarily it would seem a terrrible idea to place a concrete and glass box, ten stories high and as big as a football field, across the middle of a lovely ravine leading into the Chattahoochee River. This is precisely what was done with the IBM building, and the results were wonderful. This massive building spanning the dammed-up ravine increases rather than diminishes the site's drama and provides a stunning lesson in the benefits of breaking the rules.

Though IBM does not exactly welcome the public, architecture buffs can visit briefly without being asked to leave by the large security force. Unfortunately, IBM's growing space needs eventually required a second building on the site. This one, identical to the first in appearance but set at a right angle to it, has tipped the balance and obliterated much of the delicate relationship the original building enjoyed with the landscape.

Cobb County's primary landmark is not its courthouse but the **BIG CHICKEN (9)**, US 41 at Roswell Street, a fast-food restaurant originally called the Chick Chuck N' Shake but now run by Kentucky Fried Chicken. At press time, the Big Chicken was under threat of demolition. Downtown Marietta and its civic buildings were bypassed years ago by the county's phenomenal Eastward and Southerly growth. As a result, the square and the historic district have a small-town ambience despite

Marietta's status as the seat of one of the nation's fastest growing counties. The price paid for maintaining this old-town character is a degree of irrelevance to daily life. Unless one has a traffic ticket to pay or has been called for jury duty, there is little need to go downtown. A resident could live for years in Cobb County without ever seeing the square, but the visitor should not make this mistake. The Welcome Center, housed is one of the rehabilitated warehouses along the railroad, generously furnishes tour maps that describe the historic commercial buildings on the square, industrial buildings along the old railroad line, and houses in the residential district along Church and Cherokee Streets. It's easy to get there from Atlanta; just take a left at the Big Chicken.

For information contact:
MARIETTA WELCOME CENTER **(10),** *4 Depot Street, Marietta, GA 30060; telephone (404) 429-1115.*

FIRST BAPTIST CHURCH (11)

148 Church Street NE.
Telephone: (404) 424-8326
Open for services
No admission fee.
Handicapped accessible
Architect: Unknown
Age: Built in1892
Style: Mixed Romanesque
   Revival and Gothic Revival

First Baptist Church

The oldest building of the First Baptist Church complex is an unusual structure with entire facades sheathed in marble and granite. The building combines Gothic and Romanesque motifs and perhaps some Byzantine touches to achieve an original effect. A deliberately picturesque massing flanks the three-gabled entry with a tall flat-topped tower and a short peaked one. These elements screen the large center gable of the sanctuary. Pointed Gothic and round Romanesque arches are used almost interchangeably across the facades. Inside, the sanctuary is simple, plain, and dignified. Unadorned walls and a sloping floor focus the attention on the service rather than the interior design.

North Georgia

Cartersville (Bartow County)

For information contact:
Cartersville-Bartow County Tourism Council, 16 W. Main Street, P.O. Box
200397, Cartersville, GA 30120; telephone (706) 387-1357.

ETOWAH INDIAN MOUNDS (1)

813 Indian Mounds Road SW.
Telephone: (706) 387-3747
Open Tues-Sat 9:00-5:00,
Sun 2:00-5:30; closed Thanks-
giving and Christmas
Adults $1.50
Handicapped accessible
Age: This settlement was
occupied between 1000 and
1500 A.D.

Etowah Indian Mounds

The Etowah Indian Mounds is a historic site administered by the Georgia
Department of Natural Resources. The Native Americans who lived here were
part of the Mississippian Culture and enjoyed contact with groups from as far
away as Florida and the Mississippi River. The Etowah settlement dates from
1000 to 1500 A.D., flourishing roughly between the times of the Mayan and Aztec
civilizations. At its zenith it housed as many as three thousand people. That the
settlement died out around the time of Hernando De Soto's explorations in the area
is almost certainly not coincidental.

While other Indian mounds in the state were used primarily for burials, the
Etowah mounds were created with architectural intent. The large Mound A and the
smaller Mound B anchored a ceremonial plaza. Mound A is mislabeled; it is
actually a 60-foot-high truncated earthen pyramid. The half-acre level top served
as the platform for the chief's residence or temple. The pyramid provided an
impressive backdrop for ceremonies in the plaza as well as an imposing presence

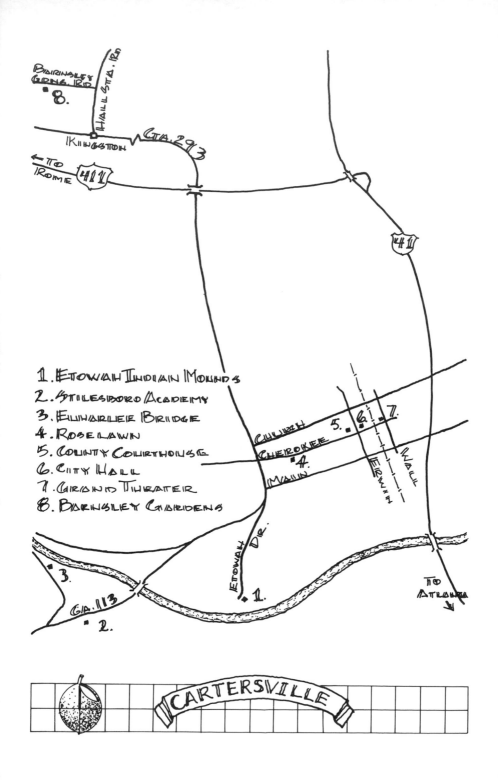

BARNSLEY GDNS. RD

8.

HALL STA. RD

Kingston   GA. 293

← TO
ROME   411

411

1. ETOWAH INDIAN MOUNDS
2. STILESBORO ACADEMY
3. EUHARLEE BRIDGE
4. ROSELAWN
5. COUNTY COURTHOUSE
6. CITY HALL
7. GRAND THEATER
8. BARNSLEY GARDENS

CHURCH   5. 6. 7.

CHEROKEE

4.

MAIN

ERWIN

WALL

ETOWAH DR.

3.

GA. 113

2.

1.

TO
ATLANTA

CARTERSVILLE

in the valley. Mound C was a burial mound and is where the famous marble statues now on display in the visitors' center were found.

The Etowah Indian Mounds Historic Site has been designated a National Historic Landmark and stands as Georgia's oldest architecture. Its strategic location alongside the Etowah River would today appear almost as pristine as it did a thousand years ago when the Indians first arrived, were it not for the overshadowing presence of the Georgia Power Company cooling towers a few miles away in Euharlee. A thousand years from now, the ruins of these gigantic totems of our civilization will probably still exist and seem as enigmatic and mysterious as the Etowah Mounds do to us.

Nearby: STILESBORO ACADEMY (2), GA 113 Southwest of Cartersville, educated students from 1859 until 1941. Now it can be seen during the annual Fall Chrysanthemum Festival, held the first Friday in November. For information call (706) 387-1357 or (706) 382-5366.

EUHARLEE COVERED BRIDGE (3) (1886) is the state's oldest such structure. Take the Euharlee Road to Covered Bridge Road.

ROSELAWN (4)

244 W. Cherokee Av.
Telephone:
(706) 386-1081
Open Mon-Fri
10:00-5:00
Adults $2.00, children
$1.00. Not handi-
capped accessible
Architect: Remodeling
by Pim & Taylor
Age: Achieved present
size in 1895
Style: A mixture of
Eastlake and Second
Empire Styles

Roselawn

Roselawn was the home of evangelist Sam Jones. It was while he was living here that the structure achieved its present form. Jones enlarged it through the unique means of lifting the original two-story house and inserting a new first floor. The front parlor features a bowed end wall and elaborate plaster crown and ceiling moldings. This room contrasts effectively with the adjoining dining room, executed in dark wood trim. Also on the first floor are a drawing room, bedroom, and central stair hall. The home's ongoing restoration was begun in 1981.

141

Nearby: Several buildings in downtown Cartersville are worth a visit. The BARTOW COUNTY COURTHOUSE (5), Cherokee at Erwin (1903; J. W. Golucke & Associates, architects), is a fine Neoclassical brick structure topped by a clock tower.

CITY HALL (6), 1 N. Erwin Street (1915; Oscar Wenderoth, supervising architect), retained much of its character during its conversion from the Post Office. It is artfully connected to the 1987 annex building (Arnold & Spiess, architects) by an open bridge. This handsome brick structure could serve as a model for sensitive infill construction. Open Mon-Fri 9:00-5:00; no admission fee; handicapped accessible.

The GRAND THEATER (7), 2 Wall Street (1928), won a Governor's Main Street Award for the quality of its rehabilitation. Telephone: (706) 386-7343; open for performances.

BARNSLEY GARDENS (8)

597 Barnsley Gardens Road, Adairsville, GA 30105
Telephone: (706) 773-7480
Open Mar 1-Nov 15 Tues-Sat 10:00-6:00, Sun 12:00-6:00; Nov 16-Feb 28
Tues-Sat 10:00-4:30, Sun 12:00-4:30
Adults $6.00, children under 11 free. Grounds are handicapped accessible
Age: Built in 1857
Style: Italianate

The legends of ghosts and curses surrounding Barnsley Gardens probably stem from its founder. Godfrey Barnsley was both a self-made Rennaissance man and a spiritualist who claimed to talk with his wife's ghost in the boxwoods. The 10,000-acre estate he named Woodlands was the site of numerous experiments with agriculture and a house designed with the latest amenities available at the time it was built.

Barnsley himself created the muscularly compact brick composition that centers on a three-story tower entry. It was executed in the then avant-garde Italianate style. In addition to stylistic innovations, he incorporated hot and cold running water and a rotisserie stove into his home. The original parterre garden design cleverly exploits its hillside location. Because the garden's plane is tilted toward the arrival path, approaching visitors as well as those already inside the house can appreciate its patterns.

A series of catastrophes culminating in a 1906 tornado left the main house in ruins. Under its current ownership, the walls have been stabilized and the gardens reclaimed, but no attempt will be made to reconstruct what has become a romantic monument to one man's enterprise.

Rome (Floyd County)

In 1834 the name Rome was literally picked out of a hat by the town's founders, who then proceeded to name seven of the surrounding hills. Nestled in the confluence of three rivers that course through north Georgia's green hills, Rome has the loveliest natural setting of any of the state's large towns. Its Between the Rivers Historic District, an area bounded by US 27 and the Etowah and Oostanaula Rivers, has buildings in various styles that date from as early as the 1850s. This district has evolved into a mixed-use residential, office, government, and commercial area with a lively restaurant trade at night.

The residential section of the historic district is a compact, genteel neighborhood that has never fallen on the hard times surburbanization has brought to similar areas in most other towns. Anchored by the mansions on E. 4th Street and E. 4th Avenue, this neighborhood extends from 2nd to 6th Avenues and from E. 1st Street to Glen Milner Boulevard.

For information contact:
Greater Rome Convention and Visitors Bureau, P.O. Box 5823, Rome, GA 30162, telephone (706) 295-5576.

CITY CLOCK (1)

E. 5th Avenue at E. 2nd Street
Visitors are not allowed inside the
clock tower. The small park sur-
rounding the tower is always open.
No admission fee
Handicapped accessible
Age: Built in 1871

The downtown area is punctuated by a half-dozen towers and spires, the most impressive of which is the handsome City Clock tower. Erected initially for reliable water storage, the City Clock tower is the kind of image-making civic landmark most communities wish for but rarely have. The rugged brick drum of the water tower and the beautifully composed clock and carillon surmounting the tower create a powerful presence atop the historic district's tallest hill.

City Clock

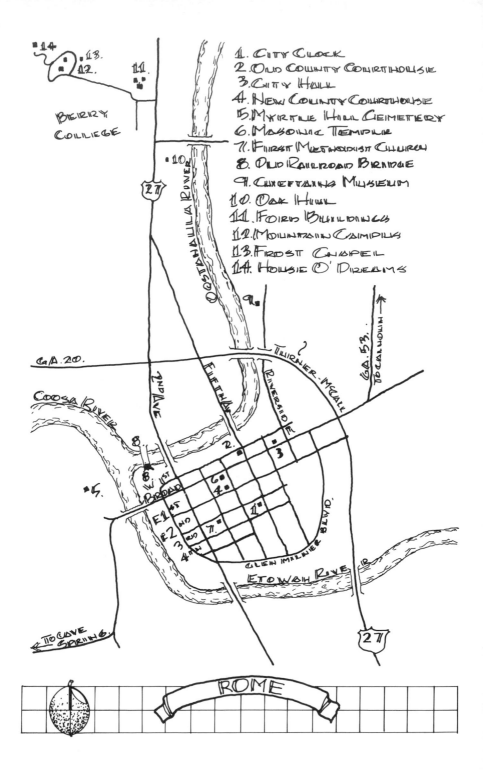

1. City Clock
2. Old County Courthouse
3. City Hall
4. New County Courthouse
5. Myrtle Hill Cemetery
6. Masonic Temple
7. First Methodist Church
8. Old Railroad Bridge
9. Chieftains Museum
10. Oak Hill
11. Ford Buildings
12. Mountain Campus
13. Frost Chapel
14. House O' Dreams

Berry College

Oostanaula River

27

GA. 20.

Coosa River

2nd Ave.

Fifth

Riverside

Turner McCall

GA. 53.
TO CALHOUN

8

8

W. 1ST
Broad

5

E 1st
E 2nd
3rd
4th

6
4

2

3

1

7

GLEN MILNER BLVD.

GLEN MILNER

Etowah River

TO CAVE SPRING

27

ROME

OLD COUNTY COURTHOUSE (2)

W. 5th Avenue at W. 1st Street
Open Mon-Sat 9:00-5:00
No admission fee. Handicapped accessible
Architects: Bruce & Morgan
Age: Built in 1892
Style: Romanesque Revival

This is one of the state's best designs by the prolific courthouse architects Bruce & Morgan. This work combines some of the elements used separately on other courthouses: muscular geometric forms, deep Romanesque arches, and sophisticated terra cotta detailing. The second-floor courtroom, now the commissioners' chamber, is also worth a look.

Nearby: CITY HALL (3), Broad Street at 6th Avenue, is perhaps better known for the Capitoline wolf statue in front given to the city by the Italian dictator Mussolini than for the eccentric, 1916 Egyptian-flavored design by A. Ten Eyck Brown. A renovation in 1989 uncovered many features lost in previous alterations. Open Mon-Fri 9:00-5:00, and for performances in the City Auditorium; no admission fee; handicapped accessible.

The NEW COUNTY COURTHOUSE (4), actually the Old Federal Courthouse, E. 4th Avenue at E. 1st Street (1896; with renovations in 1976 by Bothwell, Jenkins & Slay, architects), is an elegant, understated Neoclassical pallazzo in cream-colored brick with matching stone and terra cotta trim. The domed second-floor courtroom is handsome enough to make sitting through a day of jury selection endurable. Open Mon-Fri 9:00-5:00; no admission fee; handicapped accessible.

MYRTLE HILL CEMETERY (5), on one of Rome's seven hills, contains many Civil War graves as well as some fine monuments and statuary, including the tomb of the famous surgeon Dr. Battey. The grave of Woodrow Wilson's first wife, a Roman, is also here.

The exuberant Gothic Revival MASONIC TEMPLE (6), Broad Street at 4th Avenue, is worth seeing, as is the wonderful brickwork and woodcraft of the 1889 FIRST METHODIST CHURCH (7) (E. 3rd Avenue at E. 2nd Street).

The OLD RAILROAD BRIDGE (8), now a footbridge, is at the junction of the three rivers. Not only is the view superb, but the bridge itself with its center pivot to allow steamboats to pass, looks like it is straight out of the industrial revolution.

CHIEFTAINS MUSEUM (9)

501 Riverside Parkway. Telephone: (706) 291-9494
Open for art exhibits and for special occasions; call for hours
Style: Piedmont Plain

This was the home of Cherokee Indian leader Major Ridge. The log cabin at its core is approximately 200 years old. The house was expanded into a Piedmont Plain style building in 1828.

Nearby: CAVE SPRING (not on map) is a gentrified village which is home for the Georgia School for the Deaf, an annual crafts festival, and its namesake water source in Rolater Park. The park is open 7:00 A.M.to 9:00 P.M. all year.

BERRY COLLEGE (10-14)

Berry College was the vision of a most remarkable woman, Martha Berry. Her story is available both as a book and in a film, which can be seen at the college museum. At 27,000 acres, Berry claims to be the world's largest campus; it is certainly the state's most beautiful. A visitor would do well to stop at the museum first to become acquainted with the school and its founder (hours below).

For information contact:
Berry College, 2277 Martha Berry Boulevard, Mt. Berry Station, Rome, GA 30149, telephone: (706) 232-5374. Martha Berry Museum telephone (706) 291-1883; museum open Tues-Sat 10:00-5:00, Sun 1:00-5:00; closed holidays. Museum and grounds admission: Adults $3.00, children $1.50.

OAK HILL (10)

Address, hours, and admission fee as above
Grounds only are handicapped accessible
Age: Built in 1847
Style: Greek Revival

Adjacent to the museum is the Berry ancestral home, Oak Hill. Though an excellently preserved example of the Greek Revival style, the building is eclipsed by its own gardens; its acres of formal parterres, terraces, and lawns are all maintained with a sense of devotion to its former owner not equaled elsewhere in the state.

FORD BUILDINGS (11)

Address, telephone, and hours as above
No admission fee. Partially handicapped accessible
Architects: Coolidge & Carlson, Boston
Age: Built throughout the 1920s and into the early 1930s
Style: Gothic Revival

The central part of the Berry campus is mostly of Georgian style architecture, enhanced by a formal layout. Set apart from the Neoclassical buildings, on a hill surrounded by pastures, are the magnificent Ford Buildings. More convincingly Gothic than much of England itself, this gift from Henry Ford is a campus unto itself and another "best" for Berry: the best Gothic Revival architecture in the state. No detail was spared: there are stone tracery windows, copper spires and finials, gargoyles, reflecting pools, and acres of stonework by accomplished Italian masons who came to Berry after completing the Grove Park Inn in Asheville, North Carolina, and whose descendants still work their craft here. Of the interiors, the dining hall is easily the best. Its soaring, exposed-wood structure, set

Ford Buildings

off by ennobling inscriptions, would look quite at home in Oxford or Cambridge. Unfortunately, daily meals are no longer taken here.

MOUNTAIN CAMPUS (12)

Address, telephone, and hours as above
No admission fee. Partially handicapped accessible
Architects: The work of two firms predominates: the Boston firm Coolidge & Carlson, and Cooper & Cooper of Atlanta
Age: Buildings date primarily from the 1930s and 1940s
Style: Gothic Revival and log cabins predominate

Frost Chapel

The Mountain Campus, three miles away from the main campus, is a not-to-be-missed exercise in the picturesque. Photogenic sights dot the campus like follies

147

in an English landscape: the splashing brooks, swans, the ruggedly handsome FROST CHAPEL (13) (Cooper and Cooper, architects), the old water wheel, and even such utilitarian buildings as the gymnasium and dairy enhance this image. Possum Trot, a set of old school buildings, is maintained to show where Miss Berry first began formally educating the area's children in 1902.

Nearby: For visitors with a couple of extra hours, the HOUSE O' DREAMS (14) (Coolidge & Carlson, architects), on the crest of Lavendar Mountain, is a worthwhile excursion. Built by Berry students and alumni as a retreat for Martha Berry, the picturesque house and tower command a spectacular view over much of Northwest Georgia. Access to the House O' Dreams is limited and must be arranged in advance at the Martha Berry Museum or the house may be seen during its annual opening for Mountain Day in early October.

Gordon and Murray Counties

NEW ECHOTA (1)

Georgia Highway 225, 3 miles east of Calhoun, Route 3, Calhoun, GA 30701. Telephone: (706) 629-8151
Open Tues-Sat 9:00-5:00, Sun 2:00-5:30, closed Thanksgiving and Christmas
Adults $1.00, children $ .50
Handicapped accessible
Architects: Various builders; archeological verifications and restorations directed by Georgia Department of Natural Resources
Age: Built 1825-1838
Style: Various

Supreme Court, New Echota

The Cherokees established New Echota in 1825 to be the capital of their independent nation. The one-time bustling town was abandoned after their forced relocation march to Oklahoma in 1838, commonly called the Trail of Tears. The only building original to the site is the Worcester House of 1828. Other buildings have been moved here or are reconstructions. A modern museum telling the story of the Cherokees is on the site. New Echota has been designated a National Historic Landmark and is operated by the Georgia Department of Natural Resources.

For information contact: Georgia Department of Natural Resources, Office of Information, 270 Washington Street SW, Atlanta, GA 30334; telephone (404) 656-3530.

Vann Tavern, New Echota

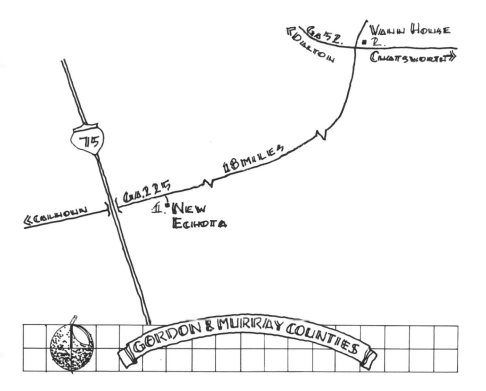

Vann House (2)

US 76 between Dalton and
Chatsworth at the intersection
of GA 225 in Murray County
(near Chatsworth)
Telephone: (706) 695-2598
Open Tues-Sat 9:00-5:00, Sun
2:00-5:30; closed Thanksgiving
and Christmas; specially deco-
rated for Christmas holidays
Donation Requested.
Not handicapped accessible
Architect: Restoration by Dr.
Henry Chandlee Forman
Age: Built in 1805; restored in 1906
Style: Federal

Vann House

This residence was built by Cherokee Indian James Vann and later occupied by his son Joseph Vann. The Vann House was the seat of a profitable plantation that included many outbuildings and worked dozens of slaves. It was reputed in its day to be the finest home in the Cherokee nation.

The Vann House is a freely interpreted version of the ordinarily restrained Federal style. Its eclectic features include the unique off-center front porch, cantilevered stair, vibrant paint schemes, and handsome fireplace surrounds. The home declined after Joseph Vann was forced to leave during the Trail of Tears relocation of the Cherokees (1838). Its restoration was executed by the State of Georgia. The house is now a museum operated by the Georgia Department of Natural Resources.

Chickamauga (Dade County)

Chickamauga was the first place in Georgia to experience the devastation the Civil War would quickly spread statewide. The inestimable horror of the famous battle at Chicamauga is relayed by the toll of 37,000 casualties and local accounts of the rivers and streams literally running red with blood.

Gordon-Lee Mansion (1)

217 Cove Road, Chickamauga, GA 30707. Telephone: (404) 375-4728
Open as a bed & breakfast; also open to visitors Memorial Day to Labor Day
Tues-Sat 12:00-5:00, Sun 2:00-5:00; open other times of the year by appointment
Adults: $3.00, children: $1.00. Not handicapped accessible

Chicamauga (Dade County)

Architect: Restoration consultant Paul Muldower
Age: Built in 1847
Style: Neoclassical

The Gordon-Lee Mansion was spared destruction in the Civil War by its status as a makeshift hospital during the battle of Chicamauga. The four massive stone pillars supporting the building's heavy entablature were installed in the early 1900s. They replaced a less imposing porch of stacked wood columns and full balcony. The big four-over-four plan with central hall is constructed of solid brick walls and heart-pine floors. The front parlor is the most interesting room historically and architecturally. Its gold leaf moldings and 12-foot ceilings were the backdrop for hundreds of amputations performed here. Pre-Civil War furnishings are used throughout.

Dr. Frank Green purchased the house and began its restoration in 1974. This project has become a labor of love that offers little chance for an economic return.

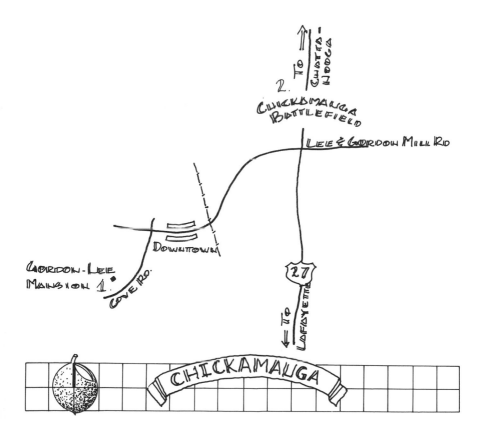

Such a long-lasting ef-
fort should at least earn
him the right to add his
name to the building's
moniker. Visitors
should suggest the
house be renamed the
Gordon-Lee-Green
house.

Gordon-Lee Mansion

Nearby: CHICKAMAUGA NATIONAL BATTLEFIELD (2), US 27 just south of Rossville, has many fine monuments to those who fought here. Open all year; no admission fee.

Gainesville (Hall County)

A tornado cut a swath through downtown Gainesville in the 1930s, leaving the city with neither a courthouse nor a city hall. President Roosevelt visited the devastated area to determine what help the federal government might give. The result of the subsequent rebuilding is that downtown Gainesville now has a fine collection of Art Deco style public and commercial buildings (a rare treat in Georgia).

For information contact:
Gainesville-Hall County Chamber of Commerce and Welcome Center, corner of Academy and Sycamore Streets, P.O. Box 374, Gainesville, GA 30503, telephone (706) 532-6206.

ROOSEVELT SQUARE (1-3)

Area bounded by Church, Green, Spring, and Main Streets
The square is always open. Buildings keep typical government hours: Mon-Fri 9:00-5:00
No admission fee. Handicapped accessible
Architects: Various

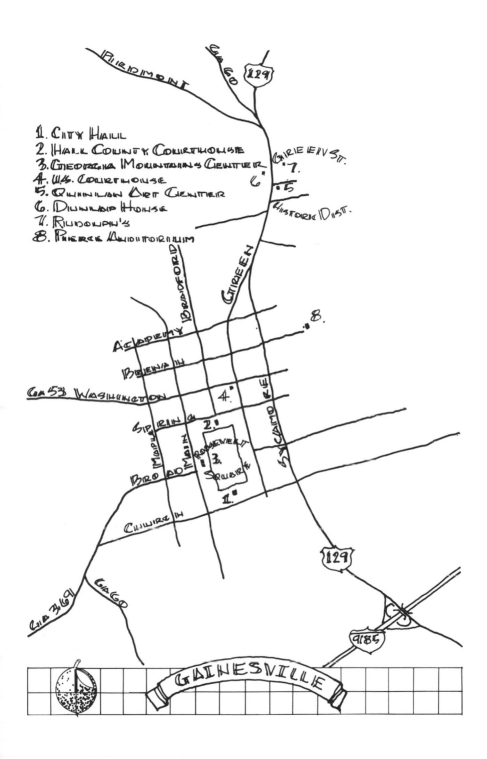

1. CITY HALL
2. HALL COUNTY COURTHOUSE
3. GEORGIA MOUNTAINS CENTER
4. U.S. COURTHOUSE
5. QUINLAN ART CENTER
6. DUNLAP HOUSE
7. RUDOLPH'S
8. PIERCE AUDITORIUM

GAINESVILLE

North Georgia

The buildings in the Art Deco style include CITY HALL (1) and the HALL COUNTY COURTHOUSE (2) (both 1937; Daniel & Beutell, architects; courthouse restored in 1976 by Jacobs, Wathan & Parker, architects), situated at opposite ends of Roosevelt Square. The Square is agreeably flanked by the contemporary brick GEORGIA MOUNTAINS CENTER (3) (an exhibit hall) and an annex building.

Nearby: One block away, at the corner of Washington and Green Streets, is the 1909 U.S. COURTHOUSE (4) (James Knox Taylor, architect), a handsome Neoclassical structure.

GREEN STREET HISTORIC DISTRICT (5-7)

Green Street between Academy Street and Piedmont Road
No admission fee. Handicapped accessible
Style: Most Victorian and Neoclassical styles are represented

The Green Street Historic District is a mile-long procession of imposing mansions dating from the 1880s-1920s. In the district's heart is the QUINLAN ART CENTER (5) at the corner of Candler Street, a good spot from which to begin a stroll down Green Street to view the mansions at your leisure. Open Mon-Fri 10:00-4:00, Sun 2:00-4:00; No admission fee. Many of the buildings have become professionals' offices. DUNLAP HOUSE (6), 635 Green Street, is a bed & breakfast inn. Telephone (706) 536-0200. RUDOLPH'S (7), 200 Green Street, is a restaurant. Telephone (706) 534-2226.

PIERCE AUDITORIUM, BRENAU COLLEGE (8)

Corner of Boulevard and Spring
Streets. Telephone: (706) 534-6299
Open throughout the school year
and for theatrical performances
No admission fee
Age: Built in 1897; renovated in
1984
Style: Second Empire style

Pierce Auditorium is a splendid centerpiece for Brenau. Its most spectacular features are the interior stained-glass panels, which artfully conceal the house lights.

Brenau College

154

Tate (Pickens County)

TATE HOUSE

Highway 53, Box 33,
Tate, GA 30177. Tele-
phone: (800) 342-7515
Restaurant open Wed-
Sun 11:00-3:00 and
6:00-10:30
No admission fee
Architect: Walker &
Weeks, Cleveland
Age: Built in 1926; res-
toration begun in 1974
by Ann & Joe Laird
Style: Neoclassical

Tate House

It was the apparently indomitable "Colonel" Sam Tate who consolidated his family's marble mining interests in Pickens County and built Georgia's only marble mansion. Not only is the exterior clad in subtle pink Etowah marble, but the floors, fountains, balusters and arbors are made of the stone as well. Exquisite craftsmanship shows off Walker & Weeks's stately design to its best advantage. Conversion to a restaurant has done the place no injury at all.

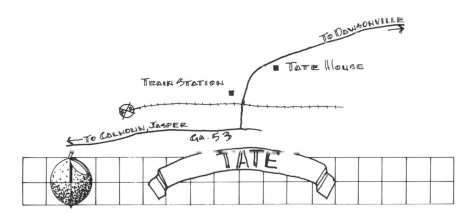

Dahlonega (Lumpkin County)

The name Dahlonega comes from the Cherokee word *tahlonega*, meaning "golden." The Federal style GOLD MUSEUM (1), in the center of the town (1836), was formerly the Lumpkin County Courthouse. It celebrates America's first gold rush, which took place here in Dahlonega. Telephone: (706) 864-3711; Open Tues-Sat 9:00-5:00, Sun 2:00-5:30; Admission fee $1.00.

Gold Museum

The downtown area has become a sort of specialty mall with craft shops and eating establishments. It bustles with tourists on Saturday and Sunday. The HALL BLOCK (2), on the north side of the square, is the oldest section.

For information contact:
Dahlonega-Lumpkin County Chamber of Commerce and Visitors Center, P. O. Box 2037, Dahlonega, GA 30533.

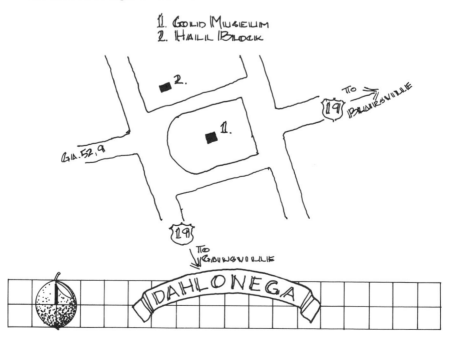

Toccoa (Stephens County)

TRAVELERS REST (1)

Route 3, Toccoa, GA 30577,
6 miles north of Toccoa on
US 123
Telephone: (706) 886-2256
Open Tues-Sat 9:00-5:00,
Sun 2:00-5:30, closed
Thanksgiving and
Christmas
Adults $1.00, children $ .50
Not handicapped accessible
Age: Core of house dates
from 1810; major enlarge-
ments were done in the
1820s and 1830s
Style: Modified Plantation
Plain

Travelers Rest

The Japanese have a word for it, *sabi*, literally meaning "rust" but understood in this context to mean rustic simplicity cultivated to a high aesthetic standard. This is what the Georgia Department of Natural Resources has achieved in its meticulous, loving restoration of this landmark from Georgia's pioneer days.

Though the earliest part of Travelers Rest dates from around 1813, it was the industrious Devereaux Jarrett who gave the house its present form in the 1830s. During its heyday, the manor was a prosperous plantation as well as a popular stop on the stagecoach line. Railroads and Reconstruction adversely affected the Jarrett family's fortunes; Travelers Rest ceased to be an inn after the Civil War but stayed in the family until 1955, when it was sold to the State of Georgia.

The palette of materials employed here is disarmingly simple: small-pane windows; masonry foundations and fireplaces; and, most importantly, untreated pine worked with an astonishing level of craftsmanship. Pine is used everywhere.

Toccoa (Stephens County)

Walls, floors, mantles, cornice, ceiling, and structure are executed with perfect economy and precision. The visitor's one regret is that an overnight stay and breakfast are no longer available.

Nearby: TOCCOA FALLS (**2**). Go through Toccoa College to get to the impressive canyon and Falls.

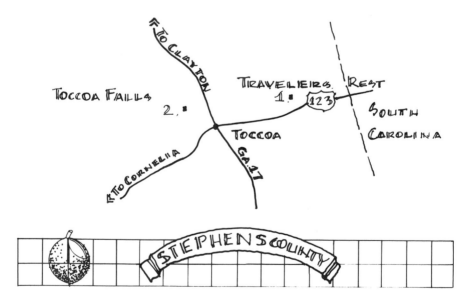

Conclusion: Architecture and Prosperity

The throwaway buildings which now litter our roadsides are more a reflection of the risk and sheer expense of construction than of a decline in culture. Even a relatively small building, such as a house, is a major financial commitment for most of us. Large buildings like the new Georgia Dome sports arena in Atlanta may indenture the entire state. It is to no one's blame then that so much building is done only to a minimum standard to satisfy such basic economic needs as shelter, industry, or merchandising, with no consideration given to architectural effect. Indeed, Georgians continue to demonstrate that when they can afford a choice, the minimum has never satisfied. The deep-rooted desire to build well has proven as tenacious as kudzu, though slower to transform the throwaway buildings.

Though rarely innovators, Georgians have been wonderfully adept at expressing themselves and their times through architecture. The simple dignity of the Federal and Plantation Plain styles of the 1810s and 1820s reflected the unpretentious character of Georgia's early prosperity. The swaggering confidence of the antebellum period, the 1840s and 1850s, is preserved in the grandeur of the Greek Revival. Though they arrived late, the Victorian styles of the 1880s and 1890s exhibit a lively expression of the state's agricultural rebound and the go-go optimism of the rising industrial and mercantile economy. The return to Classicism in the 1910s and 1920s reflected a resurgence of deeply felt traditional and conservative values. Modern architecture in the last forty years has become emblematic of the tremendous prosperity in our metropolitan areas and a definitive sign of a robust service economy.

Just as eloquently, a lack of architecture speaks of a region's poor economic health. The pre-Civil War economic panics, Reconstruction, the boll weevil, and the Great Depression all created telling gaps in the state's architectural record. A dearth of significant building in rural areas and small towns since the 1930s suggests that these areas are experiencing a prolonged and profound depression. Depressed rural areas have become such an integral part of Georgia's character that it seems incredible that the land was once considered the source of the state's wealth. The tough, inescapable conclusion is that rural and small-town Georgia has almost no disposable income for architecture and has little prospect for any. Meanwhile, Atlanta's skyline boasts of a world-class accumulation of capital. Against the backdrop of this vivid disparity, the debate over whether there are "two Georgias" seems long ago decided. The only question worth asking is why it took so long to be recognized.

As the twentieth century progresses, Atlanta has become the giant economic turbine which turns the state's economy. Greater Atlanta now accounts for almost half the state's population and sixty percent of its economic activity. Atlanta's dominance is now complete, but this was not the foreseeable outcome when the state's economy was agrarian-based. Georgia's countryside was never an arcadian

Conclusion

paradise. It took hard work and sweat in liberal proportions to improve life on the land. Today's vast expanses of fallow acreage and time-forgotten communities are evidence that for many Georgians the hope of improvement no longer exists. Ruins, faded grandeur, and poverty are often the legacy of this great economic shift.

The cause of architecture in much of the state has become a matter of conservation rather than building anew. Only pride and enlightened citizenry stand in the way of a further withering of our rich heritage. The banner has now been passed to the Georgia Trust, the Georgia Department of Natural Resources, Historic Savannah, and the dozens of local groups that commit time and money to saving buildings. These groups, and those who build beyond the minimum, have made this book possible. It is only because of them that we have this extraordinary legacy to visit, enjoy, and share with others.

Glossary

Antefix	Decorative block that conceals the end of a roof tile
Art Deco	Style popular in the 1930s; see "The Modern Movements," 115
Ashlar	Large, roughly dressed stone blocks
Barrel-vaulted	Ceiling or roof section shaped like a half-circle or a split barrel
Beaux-Arts	Style of drawing and design popularized by the school in France of the same name. Associated with late nineteenth-century and early twentieth-century Neoclassicism
Bull's-eye	A pattern of concentric circles
Cantilever	A beam or floor that projects beyond its supporting wall or column
Carpenter Gothic	A type of Gothic Revival construction distinguished by ornate woodwork
Classical	Based on the examples of architecture from ancient Greece and Rome
Clerestory	Windows or glazing placed above eye level in a wall
Coffer	Square or rectangular recess in a ceiling
Colonnade	A row or series of columns
Console	A scroll-shaped bracket
Corinthian	One of the three primary Classical orders (the others are Doric and Ionic) derived from ancient Greece for proportioning and ornamenting a building's columns and entablatures. Corinthian column capitals are the most ornate of the orders, and Corinthian proportions are the most slender
Cornice	See "Classical Elements" illustration, 88
Crenelation	A wall cap distinguished by a saw-tooth appearance, derived from medievel castles
Deconstructivism	A Modern style. See "The Modern Movements," 115

Glossary

Dentil	A block-shaped element of Classical crown moldings, derived from the part of the same name in a Doric architrave. See "Classical Elements" illustration, 88
Doric	The oldest and most severe of the three main Greek orders. See "Classical Elements" illustration, 88
Eastlake	One of the Victorian era styles, similar to the Stick style. See "The Victorian Styles," 60
Egg and dart molding	A form of Classical decoration in which an oval shape alternates with an arrow or "dart" shape
Engaged columns	Columns which are not freestanding but are instead attached to a wall and only partially exposed
Entablature	In Classical architecture, the building section supported by the columns. It consists of the frieze and the cornice. See "Classical Elements" illustration, 88
Fanlight	A glass transom over a doorway in the shape of a half-ellipse or "fan"
Faux	False
Federal	The style in architecture used primarily from the late 1700s to the 1830s and characterized by simple two-story brick or wood facades, small windows, and porches only over the doorways
Finial	A crowning detail, such as a spire, on roofs in Gothic architecture
Four-over-four	A plan configuration in which a roughly square two-story building is divided into quadrants with four rooms placed over four rooms. A central hall and stairway running the full depth of the building connects the rooms
Gable	A simple roof shape which creates a triangular end wall
Gothic Revival	Style popular between the 1830s and 1880s, characterized by steeply sloping roofs and pointed-arched windows. See "The Victorian Styles," 60
Greek Revival	The style characterized by a large front porch supported by Classical columns and most closely associated with images of the antebellum South.

Glossary

See "The Persistence of the Greek Revival," 87

High-Tech
A Modern style which celebrates machine imagery
See "The Modern Movements," 115

Infill panels
Non-loadbearing-walls used in post-and-beam construction

International style
The style that first defined Modernism. It is characterized by flat roofs and large glass areas. See "The Modern Movements," 115

Ionic
One of the three Greek orders for proportioning buildings, more slender and ornate than the Doric, but less so than the Corinthian. Ionic columns are topped by capitals with scroll-shaped ends called volutes

Italian Baroque
Classical style developed in Italy during the sixteenth and seventeenth centuries by such architects as Andrea Palladio, Giovanni Lorenzo Bernini, and Francesco Borromini

Italianate
One of the Victorian era styles characterized by segmental arched windows and Classical cornice. See "The Victorian Styles," 60

Lapped siding
Wooden boards attached horizontally to the walls of a building in such a way that the bottom of each board above overlaps the top of the board below

Late Modern
A type of Modern design popularized in the 1970s and 1980s. See "The Modern Movements," 115

Loggia
A roofed gallery behind an open arcade, especially on an upper level overlooking a courtyard

Mansard roof
A roof with a steep lower portion and a flatter upper potion. The lower portion usually has windows or French doors cut in

Modern
Architecture styles developed at the end of the nineteenth century and throughout the twentieth century. See "The Modern Movements," 115

Moderne
A Modern style developed primarily during the 1930s and characterized by streamlined effects. Associated with Art Deco. See "The Modern Movements," 115

Glossary

Molding	Decorative wood or plasterwork used to conceal construction joints, intersections of different planes, or changes in materials, typically between walls and floors or walls and ceilings
Mullion	A division between window panes
Neoclassical	Architecture styles based on the architecture of ancient Rome or Greece
Octagon style	A Victorian era style characterized by an eight-sidedgeometry. See "The Victorian Styles," 60
Order	The Classical method of proportioning buildings. See "Corinthian, "Doric," and "Ionic"
Oriel	A window which projects from the face of a building supported by a bracket or corbelling of the wall
Parapet	The portion of an exterior wall that extends above the roof
Parterre	A formal, ornamental garden with walking paths between the beds
Pendentive	The curved, roughly triangular portion of a wall that supports a dome
Peristyle	Having columns around the entire perimeter of a structure
Piedmont Plain style	A simple two-story house, usually only one room deep, especially on the second floor, and with little or no front porch. Similar to the Plantation Plain style
Piers	Columns or footings that are especially stocky in proportion
Pilaster	A thickening in a wall that lends extra stiffness to the structure
Portico	A covered entry or porch supported on at least one side by columns
Postmodern	A Modern Style developed in the 1970s and 1980s and characterized by incorporation of traditional motifs in the design. See "The Modern Movements," 115
Prostyle	Having columns only across the front

164

Glossary

Queen Anne style The most ornate of the Victorian era styles. See "The Victorian Styles," 60

Romanesque Revival The late Victorian era style characterized by large round arches and ashlar masonry, used especially in courthouse buildings of the period. The Romanesque Revival's feel for materials and ornament is seen as a precursor to the development of Modernism

Second Empire style A Victorian era style based on the buildings constructed in Paris under Napoloen II. A mansard roof is an essential element of the style. See "The Victorian Styles," 60

Shingle style An informal style associated with vacation homes. The exterior walls are primarily covered with cedar or other wood shakes

Spanish Revival An early twentieth-century style used primarily in single-family and multifamily residences characterized by clay-tile roofs, brick or stucco walls, and wrought iron

Standing-seam roof A roof covered with metal panels joined at a vertical seam, either by lapping one panel break over another or by a cap piece

Tabby A stucco-like substance for sheathing exterior walls which uses bits of sea shells as a substrate

Terra cotta A type of clay which is baked and may be glazed for added impermeability. Primary use in architecture is for roof and wall tiles

Terrazzo A concrete-like material used for floors and bases which is poured in place with colored stones or marble chips added as a decorative aggregate, then ground smooth

Two-over-two A planning arrangement in two-story houses in which two rooms are placed directly over two rooms

Vaulted Spanned by an arch or series of arches

Widow's walk A railing around the perimeter of a low-slope roof

Selected Bibliography

By far the greatest amount of information collected for this book came from site visits, materials available through local historic and tourism groups, and oral histories from individuals. The following sources, which contributed to this research, have been widely distributed and should still be available for further reading.

Atlanta Urban Design Commission. *Atlanta's Lasting Landmarks*. Atlanta: Atlanta Urban Design Commission, 1987.

Bacon, Edmund N. *The Design of Cities*. Rev. ed. New York: Viking Penguin Books, 1976. Discusses the plan of Savannah.

Bonner, James G. *A History of Georgia Architecture 1732-1860*. Athens: University of Georgia Press, 1964.

Dowling, Elizabeth Meredeth. *American Classicist: The Architecture of Philip Trammel Shutze*. New York: Rizzoli International Publications, 1989.

Davidson, William H. *Pine Log and Greek Revival*. Alexander City, AL: William H. Outlook Publishing Company, 1964.

Fletcher, Sir Banister. *A History of Architecture*. 18th rev. ed. Edited by J. C. Palmes. New York: Charles Scribner's Sons, 1975. An authoritative source on the development of the Classical orders.

Georgia Conservancy. *A Guide to the Georgia Coast*. Jacksonville, FL: Miller Press, with The Georgia Conservancy, 1984.

Gleason, David King. *Antebellum Homes in Georgia*. Baton Rouge: Louisiana State University Press, 1987. Primarily a photographic essay.

Grady, James. *Architecture of Neel Reid in Georgia*. Athens: University of Georgia Press, 1973.

Hamlin, Talbot. *Greek Revival Architecture in America*. New York: Dover Press, 1944.

Historic Savannah Foundation. *Historic Savannah*. Edited by Mary L. Morrison. Savannah: Historic Savannah Foundation, 1968. Virtually every building in Savannah is documented in this work.

Jordan, Robert H., and Puster, J. Gregg. *Courthouses in Georgia*. Norcross, GA: Harrison Company Publishers, 1984. A complete listing of Georgia's courthouses.

Linley, John. *The Georgia Catalogue*. Athens: University of Georgia Press, 1982.

_____. *Architecture of Middle Georgia: The Oconee Area*. Athens: University of Georgia Press, 1972.

Martin, Harold H. *This Happy Isle: The Story of Sea Island and the Cloister*. Sea Island, GA: Sea Island Company, 1978.

McCash, William Parton, and McCash, June Hall. *The Jekyll Island Club*.

Selected Bibliography

Southern Haven for America's Millionaires. Athens: University of Georgia Press, 1989.

Miller, J. I. D. *A Guide to the South*, Vol. 1. Atlanta: Index Publishing Company, 1911.

Mills, Lane. *Architecture of the Old South: Georgia*. Savannah: Beehive Press, 1986.

Mitchell, William R., Jr. *The Architecture of Wm. Frank McCall, Jr., FAIA*. Savannah: Gold Coast Publishing, 1985.

_____. *Landmarks. The Architecture of Thomasville and Thomas County, Georgia 1820-1980*. Thomasville: Thomasville Landmarks, Inc., 1980.

_____. *Lewis Edmund Crook, Jr. Architect 1898-1967 "A Twentieth Century Traditionalist in the Deep South."* Atlanta: The History Business, 1984.

Morrison, Mary Lane. *John S. Norris: Architect in Savannah 1846-1860*. Savannah: Beehive Press, 1980.

Nichols, Frederick Doveton. *The Architecture of Georgia*. Savannah: Beehive Press, 1976.

_____. *The Early Architecture of Georgia*. Chapel Hill: University of North Carolina Press, 1957.

Parker, J. Henry. *Classic Dictionary of Architecture*. 4th ed. New York: Sterling Publishing Company, 1986.

Rauers, Betty, and Traub, Franklin. *Sojourn in Savannah*. Savannah: Printcraft Press, 1976. Printed for the American Bicentennial.

Reps, John W. *Town Planning in Frontier America*. Princeton: Princeton University Press, 1969.

Rifkind, Carole. *A Field Guide to American Architecture*. New York: Bonanza Books, 1980.

Sinclair, Peg B. *Victorious Victorians: A Guide to the Major Architectural Styles*. New York: Holt, Rinehart & Winston, 1985.

Writers Program of the Works Progress Administration. *Georgia: The WPA Guide to its Towns and Countryside*. Columbia: University of South Carolina Press, 1990. An in-depth look at Georgia's towns and countryside, originally published in 1940.

Index

Index

Index

Index

Index

Index

Index